Y2KQ.COM

Y2K Quarterly

Y2K Quarterly
2024 Annual

Editor In Chief : Melinda Wyers

Thank you so much to everyone who submitted this year. This magazine would not exist without its contributors and donors. Y'all are the best!

ISBN: 978-1-7335707-2-5
Issues 1- 4 2024

First Print Edition: 2025

Y2KQ.COM
y2kquarterly@hotmail.com

Contents

Issue 1

Issue 2

Issue 3

Issue 4

Issue 1

Learning about the lives of French painters on Wikipedia

Craig Foster

There's been a lot of talk with supportive diagrams about how if Rose had just scooched over, Jack would have fit nicely on that floating door
and he would have lived
and she would have borne him many children;
but there has been no talk about how a rich Swede (an actual survivor of that most titan of shipwrecks) stowed a painting the size of a full sheet of plywood in the ship's cargo hold,
an actual work of art showing a nude woman with actual supple parts painted by an actual artist
who won the prestigious Prix de Rome in 1803
and was bestowed the rank of Knight by Charles X of France
and who lost a competition for a seat at the Académie des beaux-arts to Ingres, who died of pneumonia in 1867.

***

Craig M. Foster's writing has appeared or is forthcoming in Blue Mesa Review, The Masters Review, Jabberwock Review, J Journal, and The MacGuffin. His work has been nominated for the Pushcart Prize, and he was the recipient of the Masters Review Reprint Prize and the Nancy D. Hargrove Editors' Prize for Fiction.

Party's Over

Gaia Patience Veenis

My friends Jade and Ember finally convinced me to go to my first rave on a Saturday in December of '98. I'd refused multiple times before—said I was *definitely* not into that sort of thing. But get me high and buy me a ticket and I'll agree to go to a lot of places. Or at least … that version of me did.

Pretty much all I had were punk clothes, so I had to step out in something borrowed that night. Jade's blue Kikwears with tri-colored stripes down the sides paired nicely with the blue, shell-toe Adidas I'd bought for the Beastie Boys concert the three of us went to together at the Oakland Coliseum that September. My disabled father had waited on the phone for hours to get us those tickets while we were in school. I can never say my parents never did anything for me and my friends.

On the night of my first rave, my friends and I went the whole nine yards. Body glitter, party drugs, N95 masks coated with the menthol essence of Vicks VapoRub to enhance our chemically induced bliss while we danced, and all the glow-in-the-dark accoutrements. I was ready to party once I had my costume on and got a sense of the ground rules. Then we made our grand entrance at the same old-theater-turned-all-ages-venue 20 minutes south of my hometown where I had gone to my first punk shows.

Shortly after arriving I met a boy with big, curly, ginger hair and a girl with straight, brown hair in a bun.

"It's her first rave," Jade said to them proudly like she was my rave-mother.

"No way!" the boy yelled.

"That's so cool," the girl added.

I was sitting in a row of old theater seats with Ember when I felt a brand new sense of euphoria coursing through my veins and realized the ecstasy we'd purchased had kicked in.

"Can I tell you a secret?" she whispered into my ear in a childlike voice.

"What?" I responded in a similarly childlike voice.

"I really want to kiss you right now," she giggled behind a cupped hand.

"Okay," I giggled back in a moment of pure joy.

We hit the dance floor upon hearing a remix of "Enjoy the Silence" by Depeche Mode and I forgot any misgivings I had about being a raver. All those drunk punk shows that had offered me solace at this very same venue never felt *so fucking good, man*. Never mind how horrible I would feel in the morning. When we danced, our eyes were closed, except for when we smiled at each other until our eyes started rolling back in our heads again, so we closed them again. We just felt the music vibrate through our bodies in waves that spurred arms and legs and torsos to move without conscious thought. I assume it was like that for everyone I was with in those perfect moments.

The boy with big, curly, ginger hair and the girl with straight, brown hair in a bun who I'd just met also kept running into me all night. Each time they would ask how I was doing and give me water and other nice things and make sure I was having a good time. I even have a picture with them. Never saw them again in my life and have no idea what their names were. But I figured, if this is how people are at these rave things, it can't be so bad. Or so I thought.

At some point during the night I wandered off from the group and ran into my old friend with the pretty blue eyes. The one with the well-lit bedroom with French doors and an ensuite bathroom where he flushed the condom before he stopped returning my calls for a while in the fall of my freshman year. *That one.* We danced in the drum-and-bass side room. He made the shape of a heart with his hands and directed it towards me. Then we walked together to the carpeted lobby, where he put his arm around my shoulders and pointed out Lilli—the girl who convinced me to run away from home at the end of ninth grade and turned my whole world upside down for months—in a crowd near the closed concession stand.

"Look who it is," he said with a nod.

We made eye contact. She walked over and said "hi" and gave me a drag of her cigarette. It was one of those fancy cigarettes from a specialty tobacconist shop, wrapped in thick brown paper and flavored with vanilla. It was the last time I would ever see her. The night had a strange end.

***

At least my new life as a raver was fun while it lasted. The boy with the pretty blue eyes was already ensconced in this scene by the time I found my way there. And I hadn't thought I'd ever see him again. Not after the time when my mom called his parents and threatened to call the cops to stop him from making me a runaway for the second time while he was home visiting from college that one year he went.

I guess I let myself get drawn in again. Drawn back into his world. He introduced me to his girlfriend the next time I saw him after reuniting at my first rave. She was a year or so younger than me, *much* more petite than me, and he told me she was the most beautiful girl he'd ever been with. But at least he brought me and Jade and Ember to some cool parties. Like the one at a co-op in Berkeley when '98 turned to '99 and Prince's song played as the clock struck midnight. The living spaces were closed off but occasionally someone would emerge from a well-lit bedroom and return to the dark open spaces serving as dance floors punctured with neon and strobe lights.

Some months later, when the boy with the pretty blue eyes showed up at the big red box store where I worked, I thought for a fraction of a second he was finally going to confess his love to me. Until I saw his tired and sunken eyes. He waited outside until I finished my shift at 10PM.

"I don't know what to do," he said, shivering in the yellow tee-shirt and slightly askew yellow baseball cap that he wore all the time back then.

"What is it?" I said, not wanting to know.

"I owe these dealers some money. I don't know what they're gonna do to me if I don't pay. Can I borrow $150?"

I agreed like a goddamn fool and we drove to my bank's ATM.

"I'll pay you back, I promise," he said before driving me to my parents' house.

The next time I saw him, around his 21st birthday when he threw a motel party, he paid me back. With a check. A check that bounced and caused me to incur a fee on top of losing the money I'd worked about 20 hours to earn. Like a goddamn fool, I didn't even mention it when I saw him again, many months later, eyes more sunken. And seeing my old friend become so desperate wasn't enough to scare me away from those party drugs. Seeing ambulances take people away in the early morning hours of practically every massive party I attended also wasn't enough.

I just kept on raving through high school graduation and a few different retail jobs and semesters at the community college. When Jade and Ember and I made it to a massive warehouse rave about an hour away in Oakland or San Francisco after getting instructions at a map point, dressed in fantastical glittery style, then felt the euphoria of party drugs and hit the dance-floor, *I* felt like a different person for the night. Someone less detestable.

Once I ran into a friend from middle school at a rave. He'd gone on to be valedictorian of his class and got a scholarship to Berkeley. It would have been my graduating class, too, if I'd stayed at that first high school after the whole runaway incident. I was at a popular Oakland warehouse venue when our eyes met through flashing lights across the dance floor. He sauntered over, perfecting his fabulous walk, probably covered in glitter, clearly living his truth now, and clearly on the same kind of high that I was on. He hugged me and said he was happy to see me.

"I still have every Christmas card you gave me," he leaned in to say with a big smile.

My mind flashed back to jokes in my seventh-grade yearbook and shared classrooms where I must have handed him a card from a small stack of greetings for those I called friends. I'd forgotten I used to do that sort of thing.

I realized that people I knew from that darker time were rooting for me from afar and maybe I'd lied when I convinced myself *everyone* from that school hated me. So, I rooted for them back, also from afar. And luckily, just like my friend who I ran into that night, I would also eventually quit raving when it seemed things had gone too far.

One night in the new millennium, some new friends and I bought bad drugs at another massive warehouse party. Drugs that made me lay against a wall in agony and vomit all over the floor instead of moving my body all over the floor in ecstasy before melting into a cuddle puddle with whoever's nearby. The raver ethos of peace, love, unity, and respect (PLUR) was nowhere to be found that night.

I remember a group of white-gloved break-dancers striding over to the open space next to me. I looked up and managed to say, "Sorry, I just puked there," while pointing at the floor where they were standing. They looked down at me like I was gross and walked away to find another place to convene. I felt grosser than gross.

Later I heard the guy who was selling those bad drugs got stabbed in the head at the end of the night. At least we had a "sober" ride home who'd only been smoking weed all night.

That seemed like a good time to give the party drugs a rest. Because not everyone makes it out of the party alive after leaving in one of the ambulances sure to be seen in the early morning hours. I know a couple of people who didn't survive their last party. I might have wanted to join them once, too. But I'm still here. And at least it was fun while it lasted.

***

Gaia Patience Veenis is a prose writer from the North Bay Area currently residing in San Francisco and working on a memoir about her chaotic adolescence during the late 90s/ Y2K era and how she found the strength to save her own life. Her nonfiction and fiction prose has been featured in places like Airplane Reading, The Bicycle Review, and Writing Without Walls. She holds an MFA in Creative Writing from San Francisco State University and has taught English in Northern California and Northern Ireland.

It's 2006

Megan Hanlon

It's 2006 and you're living alone in a Dallas apartment the size of a coffin. Another suffocating August weekend, sticky and close.

The phone shatters the silence at exactly 1:25 a.m. It's not your cell. It's your home phone, a number which few people know and even fewer use. From somewhere inside your restless almost-sleep, you wonder what the ringing is and why it sounds like a telephone. What a cruel trick someone is playing so late at night.

You stir and search for the big red digital numbers, which read a bleary 1:34. Your clock is nine minutes fast, so the days go by quicker.

You know these calls. They come from four hours away, and even if you answer, you know there's nothing you can do. These are calls to remind you that your mother is dying, slowly and reluctantly.

The last call broke you at roughly 3:30 a.m. on a frosty morning in February. Possible heart attack. Intensive care. Congestive heart failure. 76 pounds.

Less than a week later, they sent her home. Even the doctors don't know why she's still alive.

Your tape-fed answering machine kicks on with a click, followed by the sound of mumbling. You hear only indistinct noise, can't tell if the voice is male or female, strong or struggling. A few seconds later, silence.

Then you hide in bed, weighing whether you want to listen to the message. Chances are good it would deliver only bad news. And what could you do at this hour of the morning, at this distance away, at this point in your lives?

Nothing.

You can only watch as her body shrinks and fails, and remember that this brittle, bent person with tubes and wires poking into paper skin is what's left of your mother. You can stare love at her as she begs you to pick her up a cheap pack of Swisher Sweets cigarillos, she's dying for a smoke, those bastards took hers away again - then calls you a heartless, ungrateful daughter for refusing.

You can pray for health, or for release. You can sit. You can wait.

Several minutes slink by before you decide that knowing beats however your imagination will torture you in the coming hours.

You walk three steps across the dark living room and press the blue button beneath the blinking red light. A slightly slurred voice says to you, "Hi Steve, if you get a chance give me a call today or tomorrow..."

The caller ID on your cordless handset displays a name you don't recognize - but in a different way than you don't recognize your mom. One is foreign and sad, the other is a long dead-end road, but sometimes you are not sure which is which.

Still, relief wraps you in a small threadbare blanket. The calls will come. You sit. And you wait.

***

Megan Hanlon is a podcast producer who sometimes writes. Her words have appeared in Write or Die Magazine, Variant Literature, Gordon Square Review, and other publications both online and print. Her blog, Sugar Pig, is known for relentlessly honest essays that are equal parts tragedy and comedy.

Michelle Branch at 3:37 AM

Bryan Vale

if i could write honestly and perform justly,
if i could demonstrate my paths and duplicate my vulnerability,
if i could strike the chords of apparent availability,
if i could just breathe,
if i could reconstitute my amber-frozen mind in the form of a feeling,
if i could restructure my slow-pumping heart in the clear light of southern california,
if i could reevaluate my demons and revoke my disavowals of love,
if i could surf the web of time that encloses my spirit,
if i could point out the protocols of legal emotion and define the rules of saintly games,
if i could prophesy the beating heart of a chick flick protagonist,
if i could measure and weigh the curvature of the arc of said protagonist,
if i could deify trinities of tones instead of fury,
if i could proclaim humanity instead of projecting toxicity,
if i could reclaim what could have been past, taking
        a spirit room in a paper hotel on the way to doing so,
if i could sanctify what is not yet gone,
if i could signify the approaching dawn,

then i could be like Michelle Branch,
tall like a tower, strong like a fence,
crashing like waves onto reality,
recording chords of truth,
a soundtrack, a guidepost, voiceover
for a trailer for a world made new in an eye-blink —

***

Bryan Vale is a writer from the San Francisco Bay Area. His fiction and poetry have appeared in several journals, including Quibble, Constellations, All Existing Literary Magazine, and Boats Against the Current. His work has been nominated for "The Best of the Net," and he has read for the memoir journal Five Minutes. Of interest to Y2K fans: he is the creator of simpletypewriter.com. Learn more at bryanvalewriter.com, or follow Bryan on Twitter and Instagram at @bryanvalewriter.

The fall of 1999

Shana Hammaker

In the fall of 1999, I was faced with three potential apocalypses: personal financial ruin, the violent destruction of my family, and a literal, global apocalypse. Only one was probable: personal financial ruin. Guess which one I mostly ignored? Yep! When you and your family live in a trailer park, and you and your partner both work part-time at Olive Garden, personal financial ruin is basically an inevitability. It doesn't really matter how well you budget your meager resources.

I never expected to live long enough to see the New Millennium. But there I was —we all were— at the cusp of it. I had reached the age of twenty-three, breath held tight in my chest, teeth clenched, fists balled. I had a partner (Tony) who I loved and feared would destroy me and a beautiful toddler (Meredith) who I loved and feared I would destroy.

The Old Millennium was dying and the New Millennium was dawning. Everyone everywhere frantically consulted their astrological charts, their tarot cards, their psychics, and their priests for guidance. The air crackled with excitement, or was it portent?
Nostradamus wrote about the end of the Millennium. He wrote about mysterious threats in cryptic quatrains. Then he shuffled those quatrains and threw them in the air and died before they floated to the ground. From his grave he wailed to future generations:
"Good luck figuring those out!"

In 1999 if I were to write quatrains about the apocalypses threatening me they'd be far more prosaic than the ones Nostradamus wrote.

No Gas and No Diapers
They had our paychecks already.
Fucking boss hid them with a smirk.
"No gas!,“ I screamed. "Diapers?! Won't work!"
Life lived on the edge: unsteady.

Ever since I'd heard the stories about the cocaine-fueled bonfire parties Mark threw for the front of the house staff at his ranch I couldn't look him directly in the eye. He must have sensed my discomfort because he stared with even more intensity now.
"I can't pay you early, Shana, you know that."
"It's just a day, though. It's right there on your desk!,“ I pleaded with his nose.
"It doesn't matter."
I shifted Meredith from my right hip to my left. "We have ten dollars, Mark. The car's on fumes and the diaper on this baby's ass is the last one. Have some compassion."
He twisted his mouth into a sneer. "No."
I drew in a deep breath. Tony waited for us in the car outside. There was an eighty percent chance that he was chain smoking and a one hundred percent chance that he was furious at the hold up.
"Then don't expect Tony to come in tomorrow morning because I'm buying diapers on our way home."
Mark swiveled his chair back to face his desk.
"Tony can find a new job if he doesn't clock in by eight," he said before moving the envelope of paychecks into his drawer and locking it.
I stared daggers at his back before turning on my heel and storming out of his office. Angry tears streamed down my cheeks.
"Shana!"

Dandria, a server, called out to me as I crossed through the bar. Meredith squirmed in my arms and I knew why: on days when we picked their dad up after work we would wait for him here and Luke, the daytime bartender, would give Meredith a piece of biscotti to gnaw on. Sometimes, if he was in a particularly jovial mood, Luke would throw in a bowl of grated Romano cheese, as well.
"Stop it, Meredith, we're not here to eat."
Meredith bristled at the irritation in my voice.
Dandria approached with a twenty-dollar bill in hand. "I'm sorry Mark's such a dick. You can pay me back whenever."

My mouth dropped open. Dandria and I almost never spoke to one another. We were both technically front of the house staff, but she was a server (read: cool) and I was carry-out (read: not). Her generosity was astonishing.

"Th-thank you," I stammered.

She walked away before I finished speaking.

In the fall of 1999, I was a student at Owens State Community College in Toledo, Ohio. I had earned my GED and was nearing completion of my associates degree. I lived and co-parented with a man that I met when I was a homeless seventeen-year-old. Tony had started out as an exciting lover but never morphed into a good life partner. Everything about our lives together felt tenuous and desperate.

The Old Millennium was dying. The New Millennium was dawning. And I didn't think I was ready for it.

I spent my days mentally composing quatrains for every one of the doomed futures I foresaw. There were quatrains for me flunking out of school, for Meredith starving to death, for our return to the gutter, and for me and Meredith's bloody murders.

Meredith Woke Him up From a Nap
Blood pools on a toddler-sized bed.
Blood drips from a toddler-sized fist.
Horror in my chest as we kissed.
It's a fantasy that I dread.

I envisioned myself scrawling these quatrains on college-ruled notebook paper that I cut into tiny squares, then gathering all the squares and flinging them up at the trailer's low ceiling. I watched them float lazily down to the worn carpet. It took too long. Maybe Nostradamus's spirit kept them aloft? I had time in my fantasy to swallow two fistfuls of aspirin before the quatrains settled on the floor. I collapsed among them.

I could never see past that point. There was no future for me or my family. And, if Nostradamus was to be believed, there was no future for anyone else, either. The Old Millennium was dying. The New Millennium was dawning. Or was it?

On a rainy Tuesday in early September, I found myself alone in Books a Million. My English lit professor had cancelled class at the last minute, Tony was at work, and I had an hour and a half before I was due to pick up Meredith from daycare. Unstructured free time! I felt a little at loose ends and roamed the store aimlessly, sipping from a seventy-five-cent gas station cappuccino. I eventually meandered over to the occult section. Back in the day, most of my bookstore excursions wound up there. In the pre-Amazon-dot-com era of book shopping, book sellers played fast and loose with categorizations, and nowhere was this more evident than in the occult section. Most subject categories aren't up for debate. History sections only contain books on history, westerns would never be shelved with romance, and you won't find Stephen King novels in the travel section. But it's not so cut and dry in the occult section. There, you might find an anthropological text on folk Catholicism shelved alongside Rachel Pollack's 78 Degrees of Wisdom, and above a shelf full of Big Foot erotica. You never knew what you'd find. I loved the chaos of it all.

That afternoon, in that occult section, one book figuratively leapt off the shelf at me: Nostradamus 1999: Who Will Survive? By Stefan Paulus. I read the title three times in succession, my heart beating faster with each reread. I'd heard of Nostradamus, of course. He was that long-dead European soothsayer. But I didn't know he had written anything about the current day, or about anything that was relevant to me.

1999: Who will survive?

The familiar nightmare film of death and destruction flickered behind my eyes. I saw the hastily scrawled poems —quatrains of starvation, murder, and despair— fluttering down around my prone body while Tony towered above me with a knife held aloft. The scene ended the way it always did: in blackness. No future.

1999: Who will survive?

The book cost $19.95. We had $23.54 in our bank account, a half tank of gas, and three packs of cigarettes between us. Payday was the day after tomorrow. We'd make it. I bought the book.

My obsession was immediate. I drove straight to the daycare center downtown, planning to read in the parking lot until naptime was over. But I couldn't wait until then. I drove with the steering wheel in one hand and the open book in the other, reading snippets at each traffic light. Though I'd never read a single one of his prophesies previously, I felt a sudden burning need for Nostradamus's wisdom. He knew who would survive to see the New Millennium. He knew if my family would make it.

Would we eke out something resembling a decent living? Or would we become homeless again, this time with a toddler?

Would I be forced out of college?

Would Tony kill us all?

Whenever I tried to divine my future all I saw was a black void. Nostradamus would know, and this book would tell me. I trusted it. I pulled into the daycare's parking lot. I had thirty-four minutes of freedom left to read. I killed the engine, reclined my seat, and dove in.

And was immediately disappointed. Nostradamus had nothing to say about my future, at least not mine, specifically. He had, though, written a whole series of quatrains about a comet that he predicted would hit Earth in the final days of 1999, effectively wiping out humanity.

But.

If we were all doomed, I wouldn't have to worry about money anymore. Nor would it matter if I successfully earned my college degree. Likewise, I didn't see any reason to devote headspace to worrying about my partner killing me and our child if all of humanity was doomed, anyway. Suddenly I understood the promise of Nostradamus's prophesies. I was unshackled. I had nothing to fear. Nothing, that is, except the King of Terror itself—the comet.

I checked the car's clock. Naptime was over. I dog-eared my page and went to retrieve my kid.

I read Nostradamus 1999 three times over in its entirety between September and November 1999. I studied it in exhaustive detail, annotating the pages and bookmarking important sections. I talked about it to Tony daily, though I could tell he only half-listened. Tony wasn't worried about the future. Ours, or anyone else's, for that matter. Tony only lived for his next high. Anything beyond that was meaningless.

It didn't matter anyway. I didn't need Tony's help. I had that Nostradamus book memorized, forwards and backwards. At night in bed, the nightmare fantasy that played through my head changed. I still scrawled doomsday quatrains on college-ruled notebook paper, cut them up and threw them at the ceiling. They still floated unnaturally slowly down around me. But now, instead of them foretelling futures in which we starved to death, or futures in which we slept on the sidewalk, or futures in which Tony chopped me and Meredith into bits, it was nothing but comets colliding with the Earth, triggering earthquakes and tidal waves, and fires that engulfed whole continents.

My individual family's doom was too much to bear. But humanity's collective doom was somehow manageable. I clung to that, took it into my heart, and worried over it. It became my lifeline. It softened the edges of Tony's threats and took the sting out of debit card declines.

While the rest of the world was consumed by Y2K and fears of a digital demise, I planned for the coming apocalypse. The Old Millennium was dying and there would be no New Millennium if the King of Terror could help it.

I woke before Meredith and Tony on January first, 2000. I yawned and stretched. Puffs of my breath hung in the air. Our trailer's little furnace struggled to keep the temperature above freezing. I brewed a pot of coffee and checked the TV and the computer. Both still worked. The car started without issue. There was no comet on the horizon. No digital demise.

My future wasn't rosy or black. It was whatever I had the creativity and the stamina to make it to be. I listened to Tony snore, and dreamed of something better."

***

Shana remains shocked to still be here. Her work can be found on Amazon,and includes a few more memoirs. She can be found in Austin TX and on Twitter @LiteraryGrrrl

Bess Is in Love

Jessica Klimesh

Bess is in love and stares at the clouds when she, Annie, and I are outside on break. Such a beautiful day, Bess says. Annie shivers. I mention it's starting to rain.

Bess is in love and talks about leaving this dead-end job and moving to Indiana, where he is. She doesn't tell Annie and me his name at first, just says my boyfriend.

Bess is in love, and they talk on the phone every night. Then at work the next day, while others discuss stockpiling beans and other Y2K prep, Bess tells Annie and me vague bits and pieces more, finally tells us his name: Kevin. She says the name lightly, as if it were glass, breakable.

Bess is in love, and when she tells us he served in Desert Storm, I say Ooh, an older man, just teasing. I picture Kevin tall, football-player strong, with a bit of blond fuzz on the top of his head. He's not that much older, Bess says nebulously, but doesn't offer details, doesn't have a picture to show us.

Bess is in love, and I think of the girls I knew in high school like her, the girls who were both quiet and loud in their awkwardness, who just wanted to be loved. I didn't blame them, and I don't blame Bess either.

Bess is in love, and the year 2000 comes and the world doesn't end. We're still the youngest ones at the warehouse, the only college kids, but now Bess wears a little blush, some lipstick. Her acne clears up, and her hair looks less greasy, more styled. When Annie and I ask how Kevin is, she grins, glows. But if we ask how they met, where he works, or what he does for fun, she looks at her feet. He loves me, is all she says.

Bess is in love, and I feel a touch of jealousy when she talks about Kevin. I've only had two boyfriends, and only one that counted, and that ended after just a few months. Annie hates men and tells me I'm lucky to be single. Men are such a hassle. You're better off without 'em, she says.

Bess is in love and doesn't want to go out with us one night after work. Annie says Oh come on! And I say, Yeah, it won't be as fun without you. But Bess says that Kevin is going to call at eight. Annie rolls her eyes. Oh, he can just wait, she says.

Bess is in love and crying when she comes into work the next day, her eyes puffy, her voice raw from screaming all night on the phone with Kevin. He was super pissed I wasn't home when he called, she says. Annie and I exchange glances and Annie says that's his problem, not Bess's, but Bess waves her off, says she should have known better. If I were there, she says, he wouldn't have to worry.

Bess is in love and says that Annie and I don't understand since neither of us has ever had a serious relationship. We don't argue, and soon Bess is all smiles again, telling Annie and me how they talked for two, three, or four hours the night before.

Bess is in love, and she's been saying she's going to do it, move to Indiana, to be with him, and now she's actually done it, put in her two weeks' notice, and is leaving us for real. She promises she'll write, email, but we know she won't. It'll be okay, Bess says, but Annie shakes her head, says that's what everyone always says. She still can't get over her dad leaving her mom after thirty years of marriage. In hindsight, she says, she should have seen it coming. There are always warning signs.

Bess is in love and when I suggest that he move here instead, she says he won't leave Indiana, says he can't. I feel the fury of her words, their fire, but Bess doesn't seem to. And when Annie asks how often they've gotten together in person, if he's ever even visited her, Bess looks away, her mouth twisting into an uncertain half-smile, and says Actually, we've never met, her words landing like soft pinpricked cotton. Then she looks up at the sky, says it looks like rain. Annie and I follow her gaze, squinting into the bright blueness, no clouds for miles, and say she's right, it does.

***

Jessica Klimesh is a US-based writer and editor with work forthcoming or in Cleaver, Atticus Review, trampset, Flash Frog, Bending Genres, Flash Boulevard, Club Plum Literary, Does It Have Pockets, and The Woolf, among others. Her work has been nominated for the Pushcart Prize, Best Microfiction, Best Small Fictions, and Best of the Net. Learn more at jessicaklimesh.com.

Gamers on the Cusp of a New Millennium

Jessica Gleason

After a time, it was
not unusual to have one pink
sleeping bag amid the sea of
dark greens and blues, spread
out amidst the empty soda cans
and crinkled, but half-full, chip bags
on those basement floors.

It was not unusual,
in those houses,
for the overprotective and discerning
parents to pay me no notice
as I snored away on the floor,
nestled between all of their sons.

Often, we'd hole up entire weekends
listening to Weird Al records or playing pool,
drinking a half root beer, half fruit punch
concoction we'd dubbed 'fruit beer'.

Tube TVs stacked atop one another
and side-by-side so more of us could
plug in and play until our burning
red-ringed eyes slammed closed
like worn out roller shades.

At first, I wasn't allowed to play with the boys
after dark, excluded from the late-night bonding,
because of my feminine anatomy.
But, eventually, one parent took pity on the goose,
letting me stay with all those ducks.

Some of those parents took me in,

as one of their own,
accepting that I was awkward and boyish,
assuming I'd be no trouble.
And, I wasn't, not at first, not for years.

Did I kiss a few of them?
After I noticed they were boys,
absolutely. That never really changed
our dynamics. It wasn't unusual
to find us, still, button mashing
well into the night,
sleeping in innocent clumps
and caring only for composite
s-video and darkened rooms,
sinister enough for the parasites
stopping Leon Kennedy
from rescuing Ashley Graham
to thrill us in ways I've never
been able to recreate since those
easier, socially awkward, days.

Hawaiian-Italian author, Jessica Gleason, is a lover of horror and fantasy in their various shapes and forms and can usually be found penning gory tales deep into the night. She enjoys painting monsters with acrylics and singing a mean hair metal karaoke. Her daytime persona teaches college English and Communications in the American midwest. Her recent releases include ,The Dangerous Miss Ventriloquist,and “”The Fabulous Miss Fortune” (Evil Cookie Publishing, 2023) and “”Madison Murphy, Wisconsin Weirdo”” (Champagne Books Group, 2023). For information on her projects, follow her on Instagram (@j.g.writes) where she hosts a monthly horror writer challenge, #WeWriteHorror.
https://jgwrites.carrd.co

Owed to the Six Inches of Sidewalk Scum at the Bottom of My Pants, ca~1999 & 2024

<@Hidey>

When I found them on the sale rack at Target, I audibly squealed in joy. Really, honest to Gawd, the other lady thumbing thru the weird or one-sized in the back side-eyed me but I digress. They're absolutely perfect, dead on, so much so that I suspect a fashion designer unearthed a treasure trove of my & my sister's clothes

from somewhere around the turn of last century at a yard sale, modernized a detail or the stitching or the wash style of the denim & tossed them back out on the rack for a geriatric Millennial to get super excited over. They are pure consumer nostalgia, the wide legged denim monstrosities slightly short of a JNCO measurement that swoosh

just like then, no spandex filler or butt crack hanging out that came along later, a solid denim with the back hem scrubbed off & holding six inches of sidewalk scum. My dad coined the phrase one rainy afternoon in a world that still had both

a wall phone & dial-up, an encyclopedia set & Google. He eyeballed the water line that had crept up to my mid-calf & flatly announced that I must have every drop of spit, dip, dogshit, mud, motor oil, antifreeze & water from the sidewalk & looked at me with disgust. “”Why do you look like a bum?””” he asked in an ugly,

social control way he was so very good at. These are the DeLiA*s pants of catalog lore, the clothes that fit Ali Brothers & no one else EXCEPT they actually make my size this time. The front pockets are useless & can hold chapstick or a pen or a lighter

(this is me, both then & now) but not all three at once plus - & this is why I suspect these time machine pants were a yard sale find, revised - the pockets poke out the top edge so perfectly. Anyone in the late 90s with a FUPA could not escape the constant reminder of bones-over-skin in magazines & on TV, the Golden Age of Groomers.

Victoria's Secret was Ghislaine Maxwell's underwear closet, heroin chic was all the rage, when Rose McGowan stared back at all of us with that mesh dress, empty eyes & wearing Marilyn Manson on her arm. When this one time at band camp & covered with rose petals but not you, you're too big to be beautiful.

Add a sprinkle of a Smashing Pumpkins or Blink 182 or Everclear or Foo Fighters or Veruca Salt t-shirt & You Are Here, standing in an office, now middle aged on Casual Friday. This is not a problem, just a matter of reality when poets have bills to pay, too. The shoes are different because adults can afford Doc Martens & Chuck Taylors melt after one wear in the rain after the 90s.

There are six inches of joyful sidewalk scum attached to the bottom of my pant legs. No one cares.

***

Heidi Taylor (@AquariusRevival) is a poet & philosopher + developer of the Mattel Aquarius. A native Kentuckian, she is a team reader for Taco Bell Quarterly (@TBQuarterly), proudly serves an IT Technician in Niagara Falls, NY, & holds an MFA of Poetry from the Naslund-Mann School of Writing (@SpaldingWriting).

Straight As

Caelyn Cobb

Aeropostale, American Eagle, Abercrombie & Fitch: I got good grades, but these were the only As that mattered. Melissa was just being nice when she leaned over during sixth grade study hall to explain the curriculum I was missing. My favorite outfit in those days was a pair of light-blue low-rise flared Mudd jeans from JC Penny and a fitted cream-colored shirt my mom used to wear in the 90s. I wore that outfit with BonneBell glitter lipgloss every Friday when Melissa and I went to the skating rink, gliding around and around hoping some boy would notice us, even though we sat and complained over styrofoam cup cappuccinos that the seventh graders all thought they were some hot shit. Over time, the bottom of my jeans became frayed and dirty from dragging underfoot, and no boys paid any more attention to me than before.

During August back-to-school shopping I could have sworn that the mall turned the air conditioning way up to make stocking up on sweaters more appealing. I had done my summer homework. At Aeropostale I filled my arms with Easter-egg polo shirts and any graphic tee that my mom didn't veto for having too sexual an innuendo on it. I picked out jeans with progressively lower rises at American Eagle; my mom would make me test each one by sitting down before we could buy them. At Abercrombie, we caught wind of the blaring pop music and cologne spilling out of the front door and decided to get a coffee at Gloria Jean's instead.

I thought I'd enter into seventh grade with the right clothes and finally get top marks. I didn't fail spectacularly but I didn't ace the game either. Maybe it was my hair, alternately clipped messily to the side with a translucent pastel butterfly or concealed under a star-patterned sky-blue bandana. (Traditional red or navy paisleys were banned by our white suburban principal, under suspicion of being gang signs.) Or maybe it was my makeup: blue eyeshadow and dark liner, all around the perimeter of my eyes. Maybe it was my personality. My real report card, of course, looked great.

I could have wallowed in my failures but I stayed strong. I went to a school dance with Melissa and left with a new crop of best friends. We met hanging out on the side of the gym while Melissa and the other girls at the top of the class flirted with boys in the middle. By the time I entered high school I was enrolled in a different system entirely, the social equivalent of one of those alternative schools where no one gets grades so as to encourage learning. We starred in the school musical and spent our lunches in the choir room. We wandered the mall together, FYE and Waldenbooks and the peasant blouse offerings of Wet Seal and Charlotte Russe. We bought twee shirts from the Delia's catalog and a rainbow of Vans and earrings so long they stretched out our earlobes. I was one of the few who knew how to put on makeup.

Suddenly we became the age when we were the ones working at the mall instead of running around it. My stepsister got a job at Abercrombie, where they tasked her with walking around the store spraying fragrance every fifteen minutes. Two friends spent a summer folding shirts at American Eagle, tormented by a store soundtrack featuring an indie hit with a refrain of the words 'again and again' again and again. On my way to meet up with them, I crashed my car into the rear end of a customer's Lexus while trying to park. I left the driver a note and wandered around vibrating from anxiety while waiting for their call. I bought my favorite tank top that day, gray with cream-colored lace on both the top and bottom, perfect for layering.

I'd like to say I became cooler when I moved away to college, a thrift store queen, an indie sleaze maven, but I just bought the same shit, the cheaper the better. I had mastered the craft: fit in, but not too much. Stand out, but not too much. In school and in life my motto became 'aim for a B.' I wasn't trying to be the best; I was just trying not to fail. Being the best was so exhausting. Other girls were wearing J. Crew and Coach and getting internships at consulting firms. I didn't want to compete. I went to my first job interview in H&M, concealing a run in my tights at the bottom of my shoe.

Today, I tell myself: it's hard to care about sustainable fashion when your rent is $2700/month. Of course I know better. My friend Amanda sews her own clothes and calls for justice in Palestine, and she has the same job as me. Last month, I bought a knockoff of something I saw on the subway from SHEIN.

The mall is just the internet today. I pay off my credit card and then I fill it up again. A credit monitoring service I signed up for sends me periodic emails about debt management. Is this adulting? How am I doing? Relax. I have a perfectly respectable credit score. The only way it's going to get any higher is if I get a bunch of new loans to pay for things like a house or a car. And I'm a Millennial, so. It's times like these I remember my mantra: just don't fail.

On my couch, scrolling social media as the sun sets, instead of doing things like dishes or laundry or dusting my bookshelves, I learn that Abercrombie is the subject of an expose doc about how they were founded by coked-up sexual harassers. American Eagle is trying to rebrand as a quality option for Millennials who shopped there as teens, and good luck to them. (They do have some coats that look cute, except for the part where they cost $250.) Aeropostale? They filed for bankruptcy in 2016. The teens have their own grading system these days and I don't get it—glazed donut, VSCO girl, cloud skin. But I don't need to understand. I'm grown up and I've stopped caring about grades.

***

Caelyn Cobb is a writer and university press editor living in Queens, NY. Her work has appeared in *The Smart Set*, *HAD*, *Longleaf Review*, *X-R-A-Y*, and elsewhere, and her novelette chapbook *Boomerang* was published in the ELJ Editions Afternoon Shorts series in 2023. She is currently writing a personal history of growing up on the girl wide web of the early 2000s. You can read more of her work at www.caelyncobb.com.

zeldawave

Siobhan Dunlop

all those
hours spent
running round
and round
some village
made of pixels
looking a lot
like peter pan.

remember
how you could
never get
past level one?
stuck smashing
vases in service of
that youthful
belief that one day
things would change.

every time
you went up
against the boss
not even
knowing how
to use weapons
you stared
failure in the eye
and learnt
unmerited tenacity.

wasn't it simple
back when

you were
bad at games
unencumbered
by expectation
and free to
make silly
mistakes?

imagine just
walking
endlessly
round one
tiny village
breaking pottery
in the hope
of a narrative
someday.

remember
how you could
never get
past level one?
stuck repeating
the same
mistakes
not even
knowing
you could
look up
the answers.

imagine that
innocence
thinking
everyone
knows how to
do everything

complete
every level
without help
just innately
understands
hyrule.

remember
how you could
never get
past level one?
you'll not
go back now
it's too late
and there's
other level ones
to defeat.

***

Siobhan Dunlop (they/them) is a UK-based poet and has published the micro-chapbook Glitching Al Pacino (Ghost City Press, 2022) and the pamphlet Syntax Error (kith books, 2023). They can be found on Twitter and Instagram as @fiendfull (and on Neopets still if you look carefully).

Issue 2

Invincibility at the Hands (Wheels) of My Zhu Zhu Pets

Bethany Cutkomp

I'm not sure why the universe has beef with hamsters to begin with, but those creatures cannot catch a break. Suffering cryptic tragedies is wired into their DNA. For example, they're always escaping the cage and getting stepped on. Becoming an all-natural chew toy for the dog. Bouncing down the stairs inside their plastic ball. Having a heart attack at the slam of the door. What I've taken away from the horror stories passed around is that hamsters are essentially fragile time bombs the moment they're birthed into this world.

The Zhu Zhu Pets were Mom's idea—fuzzy robotic rodents on wheels in place of the real deal. My friend down the street owned one that sported a radioactive shade of pink and often spun backwards in neurotic circles. Pretty hamster-coded, if you ask me. Press their patterned back, however, and they take off at random. Touch their nose and they chirp with cute catchphrases.

"Real hamsters wouldn't tolerate you handling them like that," I pointed out. "I'm sure if you did that, they'd die."

"Yes," Mom said, peeling the tape off of the packaging. "Exactly."

To a degree, that made Zhu Zhu Pets the inverse twin species to the hamster. Sturdy. Resilient. No stressful monitoring. No responsibilities. I didn't even need to remember to feed it. Powered merely by two AAA-batteries, no exterior variable could harm its mechanical composition.

My Zhu Zhu Pet had jaundiced fur with a star shaved into its back. Its name was Pipsqueak, or some dopey variation of the sort. Pipsqueak survived two tumbles down the stairs. Thump thump thump, all the way to the wood floorboards. I flipped it upright, pressed go on its star-patterned back, and off it went. Good as new.

Mom bought my older brother one, too—not that he needed one at his age. Although he's graduating at the end of the year and wouldn't be caught dead playing with kiddie toys, he renamed his pet Cigarette after the smokey color of its coat and arranged activities not advertised on the box. Domino mazes. Cardboard ramps. Races against his HexBug collection. Cigarette-vs-Pipsqueak brawls contained within empty storage bins.

And when those options dulled his interest, he used my body as a track. Dragging those motorized wheels across my arms and neck tickled. It was when the route migrated to my scalp that things went downhill.

Cigarette's wheels reeled in a chunk of my hair. I shrieked, grabbing at the knot wrapped within its gears. Immortal creatures of robot-descent do not contain the sentience necessary to stop when screamed at. Cigarette rolled into reverse, spinning up a separate wad that tugged at the follicles.

"Shit, shit," my brother hissed. "Hold still. I'm pushing stop."

Fingers sifting through the nest of disaster atop my head, he pressed the button on its back.

"Here we go!" Cigarette sang, waking into motion once more. The toy rolled a thicker tangle under its belly and stopped short, motor protesting against the newfound obstruction.

Had Mom been home, we might have saved my hair, but my brother settled on teasing stubborn strands out of Cigarette's grip. I whined in protest. He shushed me. This became a dance—me ducking out of his grabby hands and him chasing after me. When it became evident that we weren't going to salvage my curls without ripping a bald spot, he cupped my wet cheeks in his palms.

"Hey, listen to me," he said. "We're gonna have to shave you free, alright? Don't cry."

Swallowing a glob of snot, I asked him to turn me into a Zhu Zhu Pet. My brother's brow furrowed. It wasn't until I pointed at the pattern on

Pipsqueak's back that he lit up and steered me toward the bathroom.

I was no hamster weakling. Leaning toward the mirror, I rubbed my velvety buzz cut, tracing the wobbly star shaved to the skin. It didn't matter if Mom screamed at us when she returned from the market. No big deal if everyone at school poked fun at me. My brother turned me invincible that morning, identical to those hardy motorized rodents of ours.

***

Bethany Cutkomp is a writer from St. Louis, Missouri. She enjoys catching chaotic vibes and bees with her bare hands. Her work appears in Ghost Parachute, trampset, The Hooghly Review, Exposed Bone, BRUISER, Alternative Milk Magazine, and more. Find her on social media at @bdcutkomp.

Bacardi Breezer

Maja Urukalo

I was born in Summer

But never loved that season much

I don't know what's about it

That always gets me susceptible

Perhaps it's the scorching weather,

The mosquitos or the sweat

There's this memory that keeps coming up
Like an old movie I've seen a thousand times

It's me & my girl friends

Chilling in a park near my house

We were twelve and used our allowance

To buy bottles of Bacardi Breezer

No one could see us, it was a small town

And lying in the itchy grass with our booze

ᛏ

We thought we were so cool and rebellious

Oh, the sweet childish naivety

ᛏ

Then we would gather the remaining of our money

To ask strangers to buy us cigarettes

ᛏ

Soaking in perfume so our parents

Couldn't smell the smoke on us

ᛏ

We pictured our future lives

Where there were no rules and bed times

ᛏ

And we could watch all the movies we wanted

And become bosses, caretakers and lovers

ᛏ

Apart from Roxy who wanted to be a mom
Nothing worked out that way

ᛏ

Parts of us already knew it
But it was fine to dream

There wasn't much to do anyway

While waiting for school to start again

And waiting and waiting and waiting

For the future to come, for the freedom

For more purpose, for not having

To hide the booze and the cigarettes

We were still friends in this future we imagined

It's been ten years since I last heard from them

Roxy didn't get to be a mom

But Alexis did

***

Maja Urukalo is a disabled and chronically ill writer based in Italy who drinks excessive amounts of coffee and thinks too much for her own good. She's an addict of literary magazines and when she has the spoons writes on her Substack newsletter (A Crip Punk) about disability and accessibility-related stuff and other existential topics. You can find her on Tumblr too (@majaurukalo).

Class of 2000

Danielle McMahon

We were promised a glistening
new millenii matrices of
discoball'd infinitum

We were promised
frosty silver lips glossed
over & metallic
shadows for our

eyes shimmering pleather &
lean limbs slender
obliques stretching up & ever
upwards for a sip of
sparkling Waterford Crystal

***

Danielle McMahon is a reformed 90's problem child.

Getting To Be Me and Generation Next Table At The Coffee House

John Grey

GETTING TO BE ME

It's five-fifteen in the morning,
January 1st, 2000.
Dawn goes from my very own private o'clock
to something for everyone.

Stars melt.
Moon's a pale disk.
Birds emerge from their cubbyholes.
Time's moved forward by song,
activity at the feeder.

Still no energy on my part,
yet I cannot just ignore myself.
I need to shave, dress, breakfast.

A hawk is perched atop a nearby light pole.

I feel like prey.
Then I rub my eyes, yawn,
wash my face.

I'm not just one more sparrow
grabbing seed.
Sorry to disappoint the raptor.

GENERATION NEXT TABLE AT THE COFFEE HOUSE

It's nothing new.
It was the same for our parents
and their parents before them.

Born with limited aspirations
and always thinking
if only...

Our only hope is a pop star.

Good-looking,
TV and magazine-cover friendly,
music freely downloadable -

we are not discriminating.

Anyone
who meets the criteria
will do. ‘

Despite everything,
we are a fan-loving
easily led people,
raised on 6h.eap sentiment,
clever with I-phones
and we really do love our beats.

***

John Grey is an Australian poet, US resident, recently published in New World Writing, North Dakota Quarterly and Lost Pilots. Latest books, "Between Two Fires", “Covert” and “Memory Outside The Head” are available through Amazon. Work upcoming in California Quarterly, Seventh Quarry, La Presa and Doubly Mad.

hot topic exclusive

Rachel B Velebny

whispering
just to see what it's like
claim no interest
only a curiosity
years of walking by
months of gathering courage

ask to cross the invisible threshold

panic when the answer is yes

what if permission
admission
is not hers

what if the black lipstick
fishnet opera gloves
what if
surely
the coolest person this side of the state
doesn't let me in

***

Rachel B Velebny is a writer and poet currently based in Barcelona. Originally from the Northwest US, she has been living and writing somewhere in Europe since 2009. Find more her work in A Thin Slice of Anxiety.

Looking Up on 9/11/01

Brandy Bell Carter

On the way to math class
The first plane.
Then the second.
A girl named Jennifer brought the news.
(We became friends later on but never discussed that morning.)
I thought she was kidding.

“Don’t say that. It isn’t funny.”

“I’m not joking.”

After class, everyone on campus gathered
Beneath the TVs suspended from the ceiling.
Looking up.
Together.
Silent.

It’s so different now
When a crisis happens,
We are all
Looking down
At our phones.
Islands of grief instead of
A continent of solidarity.
We’ve forgotten to remember that
No man is an island.

Later that afternoon
I tried to call my family,
Standing at a payphone
For a long time.
As it rang,
And rang,
And rang,

And rang,
And rang.
I never did talk to anyone I loved that day.

I lingered outside until dark,
Looking up.
Swamped with dread.
No Planes
Up there.
I never slept.

I lay in bed under the shadow
Of the TVA dam,
(All that federally-owned concrete)
Waiting for it to blow apart,
For the Tennessee River to
Sweep me away while I gazed,
Looking up
At the popcorn ceiling.

Long afterward
On the news,
People's answering machine messages
Leaked into the air.
The victims' last words and goodbyes
Recorded for their beloveds
While everyone was
Looking up
At the sky on fire in Manhattan.

***

Brandy Bell Carter is a high school English teacher in Wake Forest, NC and lives nearby with her husband and hound dog. She is inspired by the beauty of nature, bluegrass, Mary Oliver's poems, and the Psalms. Her work has been published in The Wake Forest Review. Please say hi on X @englishbcarter.

MENTAL CHANNEL SURFING: '90'S EDITION

Andrew Buckner

Initially, the lessons In how to laugh at life from Beavis & Butt-head, two of the most relatable characters of all time to the pre-teen, impressionable, hormone-driven I, The Fresh Prince of Bel Air, Roseanne, and Monstervision with Joe Bob Briggs, which aired Saturday nights on TNT, are the most brightly cast visions of the 1990's on the often faded static of my mental screen.

Then the television broadcasting my recollection turns to a packed theater. This sight summons thoughts of the first two Scream movies, with Scream II being my earliest memories of seeing a slasher film on the big screen — CD player casually smuggled into the theater playing The Notorious B.I.G's X-rated masterpiece Ready to Die over bulky headphones I passed around to my friends during the previews— as waves of anticipation for the film about to unfold, having my few friends in tow, the budding and ever-promising genres of horror and rap, two worlds where the alien, I, felt completely at home, washed over me.

(Rap always was one of the few topics that helped me to connect to my peers.)

Next, the beacon of youthful recollection catches a weird correlation: No Way Out by Puff Daddy & the Family, an album that was on such an endless loop for me in 1997 that it symbolizes my fourteenth year of life in its entirety, and weekly Sunday school classes, church congregations where I feel a weird blending of boredom, invigorated nostalgia, and humor as I now recall my Sunday school teacher, name forgotten to time, continually calling me "Andy" immediately after I tell her I don't like that variation of my name.

(As the years pass on, I realize this was an intentional mishap on behalf of the teacher.)

After the buzzy laugh track calms down, the channel changes to a series of definitive events: seeing the original Jurassic Park, my all time favorite film, at the drive-in on its opening weekend in 1993 and knowing that I will spend the rest of my life searching for a movie that even comes close to the groundbreaking rush of emotion that picture provided, hearing The Slim Shady LP by Eminem in '99 with its singular visage of dark humor, anger, and working class relatability and thinking it was the best album ever made, and going to "the dollar movie theater" in a blur of instances with my grandparents after spending an hour or two mowing their lawn, boredom, social awkwardness at school but a weird sense of liberation, the powerful brilliance of Schindler's List, Saving Private Ryan, Wayne's World, the internet being birthed and beginning to crawl on electronic legs, Nirvana, "Black Hole Sun" by Soundgarden, MTV, VHS, DVD, Ma$e, the sheer ecstasy of strolling through a video store on a Friday night with the weekend ahead and thoughts of what movies to see and downtime rolling around in your head like loose groceries in a car trunk, the sheer ecstasy of finding out that that one movie you've been wanting to see has just been returned and is ready to be rented out again, first dates with names removed, scrunchies around the arm symbolizing who you are dating, the novels of Michael Chrichton, Stephen King, John Grisham and, of course, the eternally relevant music of Tupac.

Though the television fades after these bright images to glowing yet less vivid reveries, the warm, comfortable sensation of innovation, inspiration I carried throughout the 90's strikes my mind, lifts my shoulders, and compels me to write, the only activity I was certain would help me combat my adolescent anxieties and ailments when these events were taking place and secure a name for me in the cosmos of eternity, with the curious, excited soul of a child.

***

Andrew Buckner is a multi award-winning poet, filmmaker, and screenwriter. His short dark comedy/horror script Dead Air! won Best Original Screenwriter at the fourth edition of The Hitchcock Awards.

(roughly) September 15th-22nd, 2001

<@Hidey>

Mark from High School said his suite mates
drove home and got it our Freshman year,
this absolute unit of an American flag
grand enough to communicate
Something/Everything Was Wrong
at that exact moment in time &

I don't think this timeline of Amerika will ever recover from it, really,
but

this flag spanned the outside wall, five floors up,
hung between the suitemate's window & his
weighted with beer cans at the bottom corners
working overtime as shiny, yeasty wind chimes,
beating themselves on the brick in a breeze
a Just Married! announcement
of future wars & pestilence.

I still don't know how the four of them
hung it between the two windows,
Mark's suite mates
plus Mark
plus his Palestinian roommate;
the same roommate
the University sent home
with all the other Middle Eastern exchange students
later that semester <i>for their safety</i> but you know
& I know that was a half-truth reason.

Everything was so Wrong
that housing let Old Glory wave
for roughly a week,
ending with a gentle

pat on the wrist &
we-have-to-make-you-take-it-down,
it's-a-fire-hazard, so sorry,
& not a word was uttered
about the beer cans, either.

***

Heidi Taylor (@AquariusRevival) is a poet & philosopher + developer of the Mattel Aquarius. A native Kentuckian, she is a team reader for Taco Bell Quarterly (@TBQuarterly), proudly serves an IT Technician in Niagara Falls, NY, & holds an MFA of Poetry from the Naslund-Mann School of Writing (@SpaldingWriting).

My Purple Game Boy Color

K.G. Munro

Nights spent playing Pokemon blue
In my poster cladded room
Giggling as I sat in front of my bulky TV
Trying to see my Game Boy screen,
But trying to keep it down,
Before my aunty and her cliff-shaped hair
Catch me out. Playing my purple Game Boy Color.
A plastic and fidgety device, they called it atomic,
1998 slang I guess, but it helped me beat every
gym leader, and eventually the elite four,
Thank goodness for,
The save file I erased and filled up over and over again
Thankfully it never corrupted,
I kept it in my wardrobe and sometimes under my bed
The slight jingle of the synthesized music in my head
Appears sometimes as a reminder of those days
I'll never forget when I was just a kid,
Playing games on their little Game Boy Color.

***

K.G. Munro is an author and poet. Here are a few of her writing credits: Indian Periodical, Ink Pantry, Chewers & Masticadores, The Wombat Post, Pawners Papers, Reformed Journal, FreshOutMag, The Wee Sparrow Press, Spillwords, VSANA, Scottish Book Trust, Mad In America, Earthly Comforts, FeversOfTheMind, and Humans Of The World Blog.

The Phone

Bryan Vale

It was a rounded rectangle of gray plastic with a tiny pixel-divided screen and below that the classic 12 buttons, 1 through #. It was a Tracfone, a burner, a device giving me cellular network access one prepaid card at a time. And even in the year 2007 it was many years out of date.

This cell phone was in my pocket as I trudged down Concord Boulevard, which is a wide road with a 35 mile-per-hour speed limit and sidewalks but few crosswalks. Therefore I was more or less trapped, for about half of my mile-plus route from the bus stop to home, on a stretch of sidewalk that went past a long chain-link fence bordering a park under construction.

As I walked on this stretch of sidewalk, a large dude with long hair and black baggy pants came towards me from the other direction. Trudging, I scarcely noticed him until he was yards away. I prepared myself to take awkward teenage steps around him, but as he approached I was having a hard time getting out of his way. When we were within feet of each other it became clear this was intentional. He was blocking me.

I stopped walking. I stepped left; he stepped that way. Stepped right; same. Then he said, "Watchu got in your pockets?"

The cars zipped by in the daylight. I had nothing like the energy to run or fight, and I didn't feel up to finding out if he had a blade on him, so I reached into my pocket and produced the cell phone.

He took it, squinted at it, pressed a few buttons. The screen hardly lit up enough to be seen in the sunlight. Phone in hand, he looked back at me.

"Got any money?" he asked.

"Nah," I said.

He put the phone back in my hand. "Keep it," he said. Then went on his way.

That's a true story.

***

Bryan Vale is a writer from the San Francisco Bay Area. His fiction and poetry have appeared in several journals, including Quibble, Constellations, All Existing Literary Magazine, and Boats Against the Current. His work has been nominated for "The Best of the Net," and he has read for the memoir journal Five Minutes. Of interest to Y2K fans: he is the creator of simpletypewriter.com. Learn more at bryanvalewriter.com, or follow Bryan on Twitter and Instagram at @bryanvalewriter.

Thought's on a Cruel Angel's Thesis, or: Reflecting on Neon Genesis

Chris Litsey

What to make of them,
I guess that's why some called them titans

In past lives, maybe demons in others,
Spitting fire and verse,
Commanding we not fear this desolation.

They're meant to be beautiful,
Even crashing into us.

So, why do we shake when they hover?
Fear that we will be crushed,
Like a snake beneath a heel in the garden,

Or fear that we will be unworthy,
Judged before we can draw breath?

Maybe it's just the fact that we never know
What they could be thinking,
If they even have brains at all.

And I hardly thought Angels could be cruel,
Or kind, or anything in between.

These thoughts seem so human,
The qualities of a species that can only feel,
When God had only made creatures to do before breathing life into dust.

And they hardly seem human,
All eyes and wings, feathers a flutter,

Watching all with bands of orbs,

The pressing eyes of God always on us,
Only keeping to their codes.

How could they care if we are kids--
They could never know how precious--

They only are will, controlled contained,
There is no malace or charity,
As with free will.

Only command, following,
Beginning, ending, then drifting away

From burnt cities, charred remains
Dust from the ruins dancing in the air;
The rivers of salt-soaked blood–

***

Chris Litsey is a teacher, aspiring poet, and former editor of Indiana University Purdue University Columbus's literary magazine, Talking Leaves, where you can find a few of his published works. He is a father and a lover of reading and writing, getting tattooed, and exploring museums. He lives in Muncie, Indiana, where he teaches and writes.

Meditations on Super Smash Bros.

Katherine Quevedo

The Master Hand should not be gloved,
should not slide with such grace above
the battlefield, should not benefit from
a lofty distance from melees or blasts,
should not sate its bloodlust with that
gentle touch, a puppeteer's privilege.

Who riles the soldiers unto
certain death or undoing?

What controls have I?
What special move
that the world
expects of me,
requests of me,

commands
me?

***

Katherine Quevedo was born and raised near Portland, Oregon, where she works as an analyst and lives with her husband and two sons. Her poetry has been nominated for the Pushcart Prize and Rhysling Award, and her video game poetry has appeared or is forthcoming in Sidequest, TOWER Magazine, the minison zine, Wind Guide You, and decomp journal. Her debut mini-chapbook, The Inca Weaver's Tales, is available from Sword & Kettle Press. When she isn't writing, she enjoys watching movies, playing old-school video games, singing, belly dancing, and making spreadsheets. Find her at www.katherinequevedo.com.

Issue 3

An Open Letter to Myself When I Wanted to be Sailor Moon

Margaret Emma Brandl

Dear Me,

Pep squad honestly isn't that great. The striped, pleated skirt might not really be worth it, for all the *Sailor Moon*-ness it exudes.

Your sponsor will be mean to you. She'll snap at you when you're supposed to be excused from practice, when everything hurts when you move because of fluid in your breast, and she'll put you at the very back of the formation. She'll narrow her eyes at you in the hallway, just waiting to write you up for some violation. She doesn't like the Gifted and Talented kids; you've had teachers like that. And even though you follow every rule exactly always, you'll still be afraid of her.

The other girls won't be nice. You think this will be some kind of equalizer or magical transformation—that when you put on that skirt and the top that matches, when you start waving around the red and blue pom-poms with their secret inner handles, you'll suddenly *belong* to something. But the truth is, you won't want to belong to this. You're hoping for something like instant confidence, and that's just not how it works. You're hoping that middle school will be better, that somehow the girls who weren't interested in playing with you on the playground or in your neighborhood will now think you're cool and interesting. But if you think about it, they're not nearly as cool or interesting as you're hoping they are, either. You've been learning over the last year that no one likes the things you like, that their churches are even teaching that those things are evil—*Pokemon*, *Harry Potter*, and somehow even *Sailor Moon*.

If anything, pep squad will give you a frame of reference the day you both cheer and play your snare drum at the top of the stands. In spite of all the bullying you get on the bus for carrying around your snare drum, you're going to feel infinitely more capable and—to be honest—*cooler* when you get to show off that you are a drummer. There's a reason for that; don't forget it.

The other thing pep squad will give you is the sunset and clouds of bug spray at a football game on September 11, 2001. You'll think of it and still taste the spray in your mouth, still hear the voices of other girls around you asking, "Did you hear?" in a way that will make you laugh (darkly) years later—because all day your teachers kept it from you, from the whole school, and you only found out when you got home. And while you won't be quite as scared as your mother assumes when she reads—and *writes in*—your notebook on the day you learn the word "terrorism," the idea of "saving the world" is going to get a lot more complicated. I know that's not what you really want; you're more interested in Tuxedo Mask, the idea of finally having a boyfriend. But no one in seventh grade is good enough for you—or eighth, or ninth, or all the way up until college, and even then there's going to come a day when you learn what was really going on is that you were too busy waiting to be rescued to be the heroine of your own story.

You're not wrong, wanting what you want right now. Just remember—it doesn't usually happen the way it does on TV. Your body will go through transformations, the body you already hate, and you won't have time to learn to love it before the transformations continue. You'll find your belonging, but it'll take some time, and you'll learn that even that can shift. And you'll wear that pleated skirt, but it won't give you powers.

You already have powers. In time, you'll learn how to use them.

Love,

Me

***

Margaret Emma Brandl's novella Tuscaloosa (Or, In April, Harpies) was published by Bridge Eight Press in 2021. Her fiction, creative nonfiction, and video essays have appeared in magazines such as Gulf

Coast, Yalobusha Review, River Teeth, and Moon City Review. She teaches creative writing and other English courses at Austin College in Sherman, TX.

I'm not who my CD dreamed of

Catherine Zarac

In a box from 2004
A collection of CDs
Crude pink writing across silver faces

Mix of the summer :)
Sad mix :(
Mix for my crush <3
My American Idol audition

Hardly ten songs on any
And you cringe to hear them now
They're silly, they're melodramatic, they don't have "your" sound
But the thick pink marker spelled every title out
Shamelessly.
You don't listen to that music anymore
You don't know when you stopped.

Black Eyed Peas.
Amy Lee.
Alicia Keys.
Britney Spears.

You loved your playlist so much you made it a physical thing.
You never wanted to forget.
You imagined you'd still sing along.
And you haven't forgotten the words.
Just how to sing
Shamelessly.
You don't know when you stopped.

Eminem.
Enya.
Maroon 5.
Shania.

You don’t burn discs anymore.
You don’t know when you stopped.
Just that you’re not the person your CD dreamed of.

***

Catherine Zarac is a Canadian university student who likes to write poetry even though she finds it embarrassing. When she was a kid she listened to a lot of music that she now would call, similarly, “embarrassing”. But she still enjoys Amy Lee, No Doubt, and, yes, Weezer.

In Fair Verona

Rachel Turney

I had a poster of Leonardo DiCaprio and Claire Danes in my room. It was huge, maybe five feet long and three feet wide. It was the scene of the two of them in Romeo and Juliet seeing each other through the fish tank. Some days I pretended I was Juliet seeing Romeo and some days I was Romeo seeing Juliet for the first time, ethereal beauty. I would stand up, alarmed, hand to my chest, eyes alert. I would do this while I listened to the soundtrack. There are two soundtracks for this movie. One of the popular music used in the film and one of the score. I listened to the one of the score, reenacting various scenes set to the music. This came in handy in ninth grade when I was cast as the narrator for Romeo and Juliet in the school play. I already had the entire opening monologue memorized because it is the first track on Romeo and Juliet Volume Two. I was flawless in my role.
When I was thirty-seven I visited Verona by train with my husband and made him record me performing the opening monologue in the street outside of Juliet's house. I posted it to my social media and sixteen of my ninety-nine friends on Instagram watched. One of my friend's husbands commented "Wow".

Dr. Rachel Turney is an educator and teacher trainer. Her critiques have appeared in New City Magazine. Her poetry can be seen in The Font. Her research has been published and presented in (highlights) Impact Journal, Opening Minds Conference, Women's and Gender Studies Consortium at the University of Wisconsin, Social Justice Symposium at the University of Missouri, and the International Postdoctoral Research Conference in Bangkok. Blog: turneytalks.wordpress.com

Mental Channel Surfing: 2000s Edition

Andrew Buckner

Channel changes. The television set of my recollection hisses as it welcomes a new face, decade, millennium.

The curious, excited soul of a child drifts from the summer of '99, The Slim Shady LP still on repeat, through the anxiety of high school dances, the electric mayhem of Y2K, seeing The Blair Witch Project (1999) at a local drive-in and forever adoring the ambiance of the wooded location where I first experienced this groundbreaking classic, and found footage horror as a whole exciting then testing the genre fanatic in me as the doors for such future masterpieces as Paranormal Activity (2007), Rec (2007), Cloverfield (2008), and The Fourth Kind (2009) are unapologetically kicked open with a smirk-inducing burst of adrenaline.

Channel changes to September, 2003. Meeting my future wife on our third day of part-time work at a local grocery store. In so doing, a lifetime of bliss hurriedly tears down the cobweb-laden attic of the secluded heart.

From herein, a wave of warehouse jobs, an ocean that has consumed the next twenty-plus years and counting of my life crashes down upon the once sturdy home I built of my time, creativity, responsibility, doubt. Still, my first published book of poetry, The Human Condition (2008), will come by the end of the decade to help salvage my sense of self.

Channel changes to a related station: A vision of my notebooks of hand-scribbled rhymes, edges worn from use, being summoned by an increasing obsession with rap (particularly the poetics and social consciousness of the lyrics)—an interest that makes me write more poetry, themes and rhyme schemes mirroring the music I love, and even make my own fleeting attempts at rap—an action whose public displays challenged the still painfully shy kid in me—more visible to the spectators to whom I was once a willing shadow.

Scene shifts. Story stays the same.

Eminem's The Marshall Mathers LP (2001) and The Eminem Show (2003)— two instant, endlessly replayable classics that still find their way into my thoughts and into my playlist— continue to inspire the poet in me.

***

Andrew Buckner is a multi award-winning poet, filmmaker, and screenwriter. His short dark comedy/horror script Dead Air! won Best Original Screenwriter at the fourth edition of The Hitchcock Awards.

What you missed that day you were absent from fourth grade

Kristin Gustafson

after Brad Aaron Modlin

Suzy's Tamagotchi died—
for real this time.
Her mom got tired of all of the beeping,
waterboarded it in the washing machine.
We buried it in the wood chips
under the slide at recess,
nobody was brave enough
to flush it.

We watched the Bill Nye episode about erosion,
shouted "Bill! Bill! Bill!" in the theme song
like we were Usher giving enthusiastic consent,
learned that nothing lasts forever—
not even the last days of school before summer vacation.
Not even rocks.

We passed notes all through math,
already knew the statistics for each outcome
of our cootie catchers,
the best numbers
for MASH so you didn't end
up marrying your brother
and having 39 kids.

Lunch was the usual
stock market floor.
Cosmic brownies backed every dollar.
Cardboard pizza went uneaten,
what was eaten went undigested,
and your absence was ultimately unnoted.

What you missed that day you were absent from fourth grade

***

Kristin Gustafson typically thinks she is funnier than she really is. She is one of Literary Cleveland's 2023-2024 Breakthrough Writing Residents and is working on her first full-length poetry collection about mental illness and pop culture. Her work is forthcoming or has appeared in HAD, Anti-Heroin Chic, The Bitchin' Kitsch, BULLSHIT LIT, Gone Lawn, and elsewhere.

Wake Me Up

Ann Kathryn Kelly

Wake me up when September ends, lyrics implore, beneath a lonely chord. *Twenty years have gone so fast*, and yes, I'd rather we ring out the bells of spring,
as Billie Joe sings.

But it's September once more, today *the* September day, breezy balmy blue like twenty years past, twenty years gone so fast. *The innocent can never*
last.

As witnessed that day, beamed into offices and homes across a land at one time invincible, impenetrable, beamed from a traitorous sky that rained fire and fury as screams slipped into silence to smolder
in history.

Twenty years gone so fast, and we gather in a field on this September day, an honorary air show for an appalling anniversary. We look to the sky from another remote field and wait for a roar
once more.

White-winged formation, in commemoration. Military might, silhouettes in flight, aerial achievements delight
—no-malice-no-menace-no-fright—
on this September day.

Pilots bent not on obliteration but veneration, admiration, for those who sacrifice—were sacrificed—
on that September day.

Noiseless moments tick, collective heads bow, before boom! We lift our heads skyward, eyes unblinking in a different awe, trained on Thunderbird F-16s among cumulus clouds
pillowy and pure.

The clouds that day, twenty years past, a puffy innocence that melted like cotton candy to tongue
    beneath a kidnapped sun. Gone so fast … the innocent can never
    … last.

We look above and remember those lost below a terror that tumbled, vibrations that ricocheted across a city, a country, thousands of souls. Today's crowd feels vibration in our toes, our throats,
    from a scream of steel wings.

We clap at barrel rolls as hearts beat double-time and the sky rains might and we remember when a sky
    rained agony, an azure sky turned ashen as walls crashed in our city, our hearts and guts,
    and we traded our cotton candy for boots on the ground.

An enemy from afar, those twenty years past, replaced today by an enemy
    within: our streets, our neighborhoods, our Capitol's marble halls.

Wake me up when September ends. Before September ends, I'll wake my family, my neighbors, myself. Before September ends.
    Before another January's attempted insurrection can dawn.

***

Ann Kathryn Kelly writes from New Hampshire's Seacoast region. She's an editor with Barren Magazine, a columnist with WOW! Women on Writing, and she works in the technology sector. Ann leads writing workshops for a nonprofit that offers therapeutic arts programming to people living with brain injury. Her writing has appeared in a number of literary journals. https://annkkelly.com

Teens Rebelling Against the World

Brandon Shane

I looked up at my big brother

as recruiters knocked on the door

and my mother began wailing

because we all knew

where he'd be taken,

the invasion had just begun,

seventeen writing essays

about Emily Dickinson

to shooting a machine gun

atop a vehicle made for war

before his eighteenth birthday.

and I didn't know him too well

we were born over a decade apart,

but I knew his favorite movie

was Unbreakable,

and he played Diablo 2

until the sun rose,

listened to Linkin Park

while working out

in the garage.

My sister held my hand
through the worst years,
only a few years older,
but she was bigger
and stronger than most adults,
devoured Stephen King
when she should've been
reading Goosebumps,
we'd sneak into theaters
and watch the sophisticated,
paint our nails ivory,
throw water balloons
at boyfriends
and girlfriends
of random strangers.

Pretending to be greasers
from The Outsiders,
combing our hair,
chewing gum

leaning against cars

that weren't ours,

becoming candles

that lit the dark

in each other's eyes.

ours, becoming candles that lit the dark in each other's eyes.

***

Brandon Shane is a poet and horticulturist, born in Yokosuka Japan. You can see his work in the Argyle Literary Magazine, Berlin Literary Review, Acropolis Journal, Grim & Gilded, Heimat Review, York Literary Review, The Mersey Review, Prairie Home Mag, among many others. He would later graduate from Cal State Long Beach.

The Dandy Ace

Ben Nardolilli

The bar provided a possible solution. Chris grabbed a stack of cardboard coasters from the counter and carried them over to the unstable table. It was easy to find. All Chris had to do was follow the sound of rattling dishes and glassware. The customer trying to balance them thanked Chris. He reached out to grab the coasters, but Chris insisted on fixing the problem himself. The owner claimed it was no issue. Business was slow. After he got up off the floor, Chris asked the customer if he wanted more water. He nodded. Chris looked around for Cory, who was supposed to be his server. When he was unable to find him, Chris got the pitcher, and refilled the empty glass. Chris was glad it would not spill over his meal. Everything was even and level.

"That's enough. Thanks." The customer said.

"I should get rid of these tables. We've had them too long. They're twenty years old."

"Oh, you don't need to do that. You really don't see tables like this anymore. All metal with the rim looking like it's art deco with these ridges."

"I got them because I thought they looked retro."

"They are retro now."

Chris shook his head. "Not like art deco."

"I like them."

"How's the burger?"

The customer took a bite and gave Chris a thumbs up.

"I'm Chris."

The customer finished chewing. "Richard."

"How about this, when I get around to getting new tables, I'll let you take one of these for yourself. Not a wobbly one. A good one."

"Uh, thanks "

***

When the door opened, Chris was looking at the tower going up across the street. He turned around to see who had come in. A group of young men stood in the entrance. A member of the party touched one of the exposed brick columns. The others followed suit.

"Those were big back then, right?" He asked them.

The other men in the group nodded.

Sasha, the hostess, asked if they needed to be seated. As soon as he heard her, Chris made a mental note. When there was a moment, he would tell Sasha to say "would like" instead. Need implied a kind of emergency he doubted would ever apply to their customers.

"Is this Dandy Ace?" one of them asked. Chris noticed he was wearing a t-shirt for something called the Rod Stewart Museum.

"Yes, it is," Sasha said.

"Then yeah," he said while trying to stifle a laugh. "We definitely need to be seated."

***

A couple entered the restaurant and noticed Chris' help wanted sign in the window. While they waited for a table, Chris saw them pointing to it and nodding.

"Oh, that's that font," one of them said.

"Oh my God, yeah it is."

"That ancient looking thing. The one you used to see on websites. Like every place wanted to look mysterious and old."

"He wasn't wrong."

"Papyrus!" The woman remembered. "That's it."

"Totally fits in with the theme of this place," her partner added. Sasha led them past several occupied tables and seated them under one of Chris' Jim Jarmusch posters. Chris took the water pitcher from Cory and said he would deal with the couple.

"First time here?" He asked them.

"Yes," the man said.

"I'm surprised it's this busy on a Wednesday night."

Chris smiled at the woman. "Yes, me too. Are you from the neighborhood?"

They shook their heads.

He continued. "Oh well. They've been building all kinds of things in the neighborhood. Thank God It's mostly done now. People have started moving in. I thought you might be part that. It's been good for business as you can see. It's basically us and Mancuso's for food. I think we're better though."

"Never heard of it," the man said.

"We've been here over twenty years, you know, and I've never seen anything like it. Who thought downtown Brooklyn would get this popular, this fast?"

"I can't imagine it looking any different," the woman replied.

"Well, it did. It did. We could see the Twin Towers real clear back then." Chris paused and cleared his throat. "Just as an example of what has changed, you know."

"Of course."

"Enjoy your meal. I recommend the poppers as a starter."

The couple looked at their menus. Chris overheard them discussing the options.

"He wasn't lying," the man said. "There are poppers."

"Three different kinds too! Oh damn. But can you believe it? Just like he said. No kale or avocado at all on this menu."

"Guess they weren't invented yet?" He laughed.

***

The man in the Rod Stewart Museum t-shirt returned with a different trio of friends. Sasha seated them, Cory took their order, and Chris stood behind another one of the concrete columns to hear what they had to say. What would they find interesting now? They ignored the pylon, the posters, and the poppers on the menu. They preferred to look up at stationary disco ball hanging above them, as well as the mirrors hanging on an exposed brick wall. One of them rearranged his chair so he could look at his reflection and adjust his hair. The man in the t-shirt got his other companion's attention and pointed to the corner behind Chris.

"Is that...a horse from a merry-go-round?" He laughed.

They agreed it was.

"Like just dumped into the restaurant for no reason, like it's the circus."

Chris turned around. He looked at the multicolored equine slumped against the wall. It was skewered in the middle with a brass pole in need of polishing. His brother found it at a bankruptcy auction down on the Jersey Shore. No one else bid on it. Chris wondered about how much the horse would set him back now. It was barely vintage then. Now it was positively antique.

"Hell yeah, dude," the man in the t-shirt said. "He was totally right."
Chris stepped out from behind the column and looked at the group. "Who?"
The man was startled. "What?"
"Who was totally right about this place?"
The customer who had been checking himself in the mirror answered him. "Ricky."
The man in the t-shirt shook his head. "Don't-"
"Ricky who?"
It was no use. He continued. "Ricky's got this podcast. He talked about this place.
"About the Dandy Ace?"
"Hard-on County, USA," another one of the friends added.
Chris was still confused. "He's a reviewer?"
"You don't need to do anything about it," the man in the t-shirt said. "It's okay. He wasn't saying anything bad about the place."
"Oh. Are the other people here because of it?"
He looked around. "I dunno. Maybe all the single guys?"
Chris took out his phone. "I got to listen to this."
"No, you really shouldn't. Shit, Ricky's going to be pissed. He hates when the fans do this."
"What episode is it?"
"Please, really. Don't." The music changed and the man in the t-shirt noticed it. "Oh, I know this. This is the Stokes."
Chris nodded. "Strokes."
"God, he was right about this place."
***
When Richard came in, Chris immediately stopped folding the cloth napkins. He rushed over to him, bypassing Sasha and Cory. "Please," he nearly shouted at Richard, "come this way."
"Oh, okay."
"I remember you, right? Richard."
"Yeah, yeah, I came here before."
Chris brought him to a table right between the merry-go-round horse and a pool table covered in red felt. It had no cues or balls. Richard sat down. Chris grabbed a pitcher and poured him some water. "We've

changed the menu since you came."
"Oh, okay."
"No more poppers."
"Cool."
"We have a kale Cesar now. Avocado toast."
"Uh huh."
"Unfortunately, I haven't been able to change the music yet. No Rod Stewart."
Richard put his menu down. "Look-"
"Ricky, I don't understand."
"Well, it was just this bit on the show about making up a Rod Stewart Museum because of the old joke that-"
Chris stopped him. "No, I mean what you said about the place. You dissed us. You said we're stuck in 2000, 2002. You said our food was bad, from before restaurants started getting better and looking nicer. You couldn't stop talking about that," he pointed to the horse, "without laughing. I don't get it."
" I'm sorry, man. I told the fans not to come here or cause you any issues. I really meant it as a compliment."
"A compliment? How? It sounded like you were saying the place is bad. It's old. It's bland. It's out of date, all that."
"Yeah, no, that's why I like it." Ricky took a sip of water. "I don't mind your food. I didn't want to say it was like, inedible or anything. It's just not like everywhere else these days. All these added ingredients. Plus all the geographies and philosophies that keep getting mentioned. I don't need to know about any of that. When I want a hamburger I just want a burger and not some backstory."
"Do you want a burger? Medium-rare?"
"I mean, sure. But that's not the point. The point is that, like, this place is a time capsule."
"How? We're only a couple years old. Go to Mancuso's down the block. That place is a real relic. You can't even get a Diet Coke there."
" This is vintage now."
"Now?"
"It's okay. Someday I'm gonna be vintage too. The podcast. Maybe all podcasts. Who knows how long this bullshit will last. You'll probably

last longer than us."
"Thanks."
"And it's good you're going for a millennium theme here. Party like it's 1999 and all that."
"I didn't go with anything."
"I mean, you've kept it. You know?"
"Sure."
"It's just nice. It's nice to go to a place that takes you back to that time. The way things were and also the way we thought things would be. The early days of email and searching for stuff online. Finding random people from around the world. Webrings and midi files. Counters on the bottoms of websites. No algorithms following you. All that."
"I wouldn't know. I wasn't really into computers back then."
"Well, that's the way it was. When you wanted to find a picture to, well, when you wanted to find a picture, you had to dig it up from some weird website and you had to wait for the thing to fully load, line by line. Like a damn tapestry. But it was nice. We're spoiled today."
"Sure."
"It was back when all we had to worry about was Y2K, and we would get angry over the dumbest shit instead. Tech had the answers. There was going to be a global village or something like that. The candy was getting bigger. The games kept getting better."
"I was just trying to keep this place afloat."
"Sure, sure. But for me and my fans, being here is like having that feeling again."
"Which one?"
Richard looked at the horse. "Feeling it's all over. But in a good way. No more history. Just the news. God, I sound old."
Chris smiled at Ricky, and left to put in his order for the burger.

***

Ben Nardolilli is a MFA candidate at Long Island University. His work has appeared in Perigee Magazine, Door Is a Jar, UCity Review, Red Fez, The Oklahoma Review, Quail Bell Magazine, and Slab. Follow his publishing journey at mirrorsponge.blogspot.com.

My Doctor Wants to Know What Childhood Trauma Caused My Eating Disorder

Claire Nelson

Slimfast
Snackwells
100 calorie packs
Low rise jeans
Christina Aguilera's hip bones
My mom dropping me off once a week
at Weight Watchers meetings in the Lutheran church across from Walmart
The lady at Weight Watchers who said
I should put on cherry ChapStick
if I wanted something sweet
Victoria's Secret Pink collection
Tramp stamps
Morgan Spurlock's "Supersize Me"
& footage of fat people on the news every night,
the present fear that one of the blurred faces
would be mine
Mandy Moore
Curves
The off-brand Christian Curves in the K-Mart
shopping center that my mom took us to
Running circuits for Jesus, staying lean to contemporary Christian
Fat Camp: An MTV Docs Movie Presentation
Looking up fat camps on the family computer we kept in the roll top desk in the dining room & crying
The moment in The Breakfast Club when Judd Nelson says "Claire is a fat girl's name"
My burning shame
My body

***

MyDoctorWantstoKnowWhatChildhoodTraumaCausedMyEatingDisorder

Claire Nelson is a human and poet living in the coastal empire. You can find her poems at low tide.

Ode to Jewel

Anna Dodson

Say breakfast lover. Say soul saver.
Say nite-lite in shining armor,
sounds from my daughter's room
from the record I bought at Target
at a musak kiosk.
Don't be discouraged.
when I look at the cartoon cover
with you and the guitar telling truths
and summer stories starring Sammy the Spider,
I think of long drives in the back seat,
my CD player skipping like my heart
falling apart and together.
I'll never take it back
because you were my someone, sometime.
You play a moonlit sonata.
If I were a bird, I could fly to Jupiter.
You were always the comforting one,
drinking deep and singing with a full throat of poesy
set to yodel—yell
screaming thoughts in otherwise silence.
Loneliness nothing—but misery loves company.
I guess what I'm saying is there could be worse things
than upbeat tunes for toddlers
my child has taken for her own in the back seat,
and I'd rather hear her sing than cry
so she knows life is more than endurance:
something that endears us to others.

***

Anna Dodson's poetry and prose have appeared in Occulum, Potomac Review, Per Contra, and elsewhere. She received a PhD in English from Rice University and currently works as a scientific writer in Houston, TX.

We are the Class of 2000

Jonathan Horowitz

We were told we were special. Librarians, teachers, school administrators who organize time capsule burials in the front lawns of elementary schools, our parents, MTV and Nickelodeon, children's book publishers—pretty much anyone with a meaningful connection to children born between November 1981 and October 1982—declared that we would define the lens through which future generations would analyze the past. Significant because our high school graduation would be the first in the new millennium, our class was the vanguard of the greatest generation since the Greatest Generation. We were the Class of 2000.

Yet, responsibilities in the distant future meant nothing to first graders. I was more interested in why my classmate kept getting his head stuck in his desk. These were simpler times: phys ed consisted of a gym teacher in a neon tracksuit blasting "Jump" by Van Halen while students ran circles around a basketball court. The long-term ramifications of my decisions were unimaginable. I couldn't even fathom the consequences of tossing myself from the top of a car tire pyramid onto a thin layer of garden pebbles on the playground floor (it hurt). Still, the weighty symbolism of the year 2000 etched into my mind. I learned what lay ahead through a steady diet of 80s movies on basic cable: a steadfast cyborg sent to the present on an assassination assignment to prevent the future (The Terminator), the potential for time travel to lead to inappropriate relations with your hot mom (Back to the Future), and the opportunistic cloning of hot women (Weird Science). In retrospect, such burning wants of the future were clearly desires forged in a past Boomers wouldn't let go, so our generation were to see this media as cautionary tales, wisdom to avoid the pitfalls of technology as we propelled into a new world.

No longer a swarm of snot-nosed kids tempting serious injury on dangerous playground equipment, the Class of 2000 was a vessel for America's desires. At each academic milestone, we were reminded that children are the future, that we are the last great hope of the old millennium, the first great hope of the new one, the liminal group that encompassed the gap between the Class of 1999 (Generation X) and the Class of 2001 (Millennials). The times they were a-becoming quite different. The Simpsons ruled prime time. Teenage Mutant Ninja Turtles opened our eyes to art history. MC Hammer and Vanilla Ice brought Rap to suburban talent shows. Basking in the LED glow of the car audio room at Nobody Beats the Wiz, we dreamed of Chrysler wood-paneled minivans with TVs in the back seats. CD players replaced dual cassette decks and discmen rendered Walkmen relics. We went full analog to digital, from information imprinted on easily tangled ribbons of tape to information etched by lasers onto durable, reflective round discs. Life was good. We were the Class of 2000.

Nothing shouted the future like computers. Constrained by black screens and fluorescent green text-based interfaces, the machines of the 80s were ancient, sufficing only for learning computer basics in lab class; writing papers that needed to be saved on a floppy disc, or printed, for posterity; and playing Oregon Trail, an educational game that enlightened modern children to the dangers of dysentery. Color computers arrived on the scene and changed everything. Windows and Mac OS made the digital environment wanderable, accessible, and enticing—desktop operating systems became graphical worlds with icons and images. Meanwhile, the internet arrived quietly. Before websites, there was nothing online except stock updates, banking, or educational games. I would sign in with my great uncle's unwieldy Prodigy username—BKHX67A—be confused by the gnarly sounds, be impressed by the fact I was connected to a contraption that funneled information through a phone line, and sign out. Although the internet looked like MS-DOS, I had an inkling of the possibilities. Information from anywhere in the world was accessible at home, in an instant, and available to store for posterity—again, on a plastic disc, but smaller. A revolution was brewing. The World Wide Web formed a space ripe for conquest. Distances collapsed. The world of ideas diminished through access to information. If I craved information, I no longer needed to master the Dewey decimal system and sift through hundreds of index cards in the library card catalog: I typed into Metacrawler and things appeared, things the library would never hold in its vaults. Porn in plastic bags hidden in the woods was now obsolete. The transition from analog to digital was almost complete. The Dot-com bubble kept expanding, and we were prepared for the burst. We were the Class of 2000.

Surprisingly, what had changed our lives for the better presented an unexpected, looming apocalypse: the Y2K bug. The Class of 2000 had been saviors. Now, the year 2000 was a harbinger of societal failures resulting from vanity and arrogance—why had we moved so fast? Our punishment was almost biblical. Once internal digital clocks hit 00—something impossible with analog—computers wouldn't know whether the date was 2000 or 1900. Markets would crash. Airports would lose contact with planes. Hard drives would burst into flames. Few had planned for Y2K, and those who had were ignored because the year 2000 was an abstraction, so far off. As 2000 inched nearer, Y2K panic simmered. We held our collective breath preparing for the New Year's Ball to drop. The Class of 2000 was no longer the future; it symbolized misfortune, a reset—the nil year, emptiness, a gap. Ultimately, the mirrored ball dropped without incident. 2000 ended up being just a number. The symbol of 2000 emptied and refilled instantaneously. Instead of representing the future—or nothing—the Class of 2000 represented something even worse: the past. And there was nothing we could do about it, even if we are the Class of 2000.

***

Jonathan Horowitz is an educator, muralist, and writer from Central Jersey. Currently, he develops policy and programming interventions to address health equity in communities affected by poverty, while teaching creative writing to middle-schoolers on Long Island. He completed his MFA in Fiction and Literary Translation at Columbia (LTAC) joint course of study at Columbia University. His work has appeared in Columbia Journal, Northwest Review, and Bridge Eight.

Issue 4

A Goofy Movie

Adam Shaw

The first time I watch A Goofy Movie, I'm 38 years old. My wife and daughter are out of town, and I've taken an edible, DoorDashed a piece of cheesecake, and settled into the corner of the sectional with my dogs. I have the thought that I should watch this with my daughter, not alone and a little high and a little sad, but it also fills the hole I'm waddling through given the sudden absence of a child in my home, the noise and messes and questions and more noises and more messes and more questions. Things I shouldn't miss but do. Things I worry about, talk to my therapist about.

The movie starts with Goofy's son Max setting out to win over his love interest, Roxanne, by interrupting a school assembly to perform a cover of Powerline's "Stand Up." The assembly reminds me of my own assemblies twenty years prior—kids in baggy pants, unbuttoned flannels with tee-shirts underneath, Bobby's single pierced ear. Max's Powerline-inspired getup, polarized sunglasses, a jumpsuit that cinches at the ankles and elbows. I see myself in these things, or at least a version of myself, which isn't something that happens so much when I watch movies anymore. I watch The Incredibles with my daughter and relate with the parents arguing over how to raise their kids. I watch This is 40 with my wife and relate with Paul Rudd sitting on the toilet pretending to shit so he can have a moment of silence. I watch A Goofy Movie by myself, though, and relate with the teenager because of the TV cart Bobby steals from the school media center, the camcorder P.J. records the stunt with, Max's peers watching the performance with their eyes, not their phones.

I've been thinking lately about how old I feel, how old I am, how my twentieth high school reunion is this year, how I'm closer to 50 than I am to the version of myself that watched the news coverage of 9/11 in my high school cafeteria. I think about this when my phone tells me my cheesecake is sitting on my front porch because I get up without pain given the hip replacement I had before my 37th birthday, a procedure I was young for but old enough to have done.

Not long after Max's stunt, Principal Mazur calls Goofy to tell him what Max has done. He says that Goofy should reevaluate the way he's raising his child, warns him that Max could end up in the electric chair. Goofy grapples with the uncertainty of parenthood, whether he's messed up, whether he can turn things around and provide for his son, put him in line, so he decides to protect his boy from arrest and jail and the electric chair by taking him on a fishing trip. I see this and picture the elementary schools my wife and I have been touring, the house in the 'burbs we moved to, a deed restricted community. I realize I don't know what a deed restricted community is, just that it sounds safe, the kind of place you ought to raise a kid. I think about how I have no idea what I'm doing, wonder when I would have learned to.

My sophomore year of high school, I wrote an essay on Lord of the Flies for my English class. Our family computer was the same kind of thing I imagine Max writing on—an off-white hulk of a monitor, a matching tower that hid underneath the desk, hummed at startup, beeped and ground to connect to AOL. I was failing English; later that year, Principal Beeker would call my parents to discuss my lack of academic achievement, my disciplinary issues, my inability to stay awake. The Lord of the Flies essay was my life preserver, the assignment I could use to get myself over the hump, pass the semester. I'd told my mom this, but she'd been drinking and hadn't remembered. Around midnight she stumbled into our computer room, spit a what the fuck are you doing? and leaned, maybe fell against the wall. I told her I was sorry, started to explain myself but she cut me off, reached down and unplugged the computer. When I scrambled out of the chair and toward the outlet, she shoved me away, told me to get to bed. I did. The next morning, she woke me up by hitting me with a rake, telling me not to test her again. I remember this and think that she, too, had no idea what she was doing.

In the ten minutes between Max's performance at the school assembly and Goofy telling Max about the fishing trip, Max has secured a date with Roxane to Staci's party, where they'll watch the Powerline concert on pay-per-view; heard his name chanted by the student body in front of the school; and danced/sang/skateboarded his way home. He no longer feels outcast; he no longer worries about impressing the girl. What Max hears when Goofy breaks the news, then, isn't that he's going on a fishing trip with his dad, but that he's losing everything he's gained since his performance earlier that day. It's around this time that I realize 1.) that I've already eaten most of the cheesecake I ordered to last the movie, and 2.) that the closeness I'd felt with Max, the relationship I'd shared, is gone. I try to bring it back by remembering myself in Max's shoes, remembering Sara O'Neill inviting me to Warped Tour one summer, the feeling that my future hinged on how it went, that whether she held my hand leaned against me or kissed me mattered more the SATs, college admissions, working an extra shift to buy my first cell phone.

I remember it but don't relate to it. Or maybe I can relate to it but choose not to.

I still own the copy of Lord of the Flies that I read in English class. I own the AOL CD I used on our old computer, too. I own a windbreaker that cinches at the waist and wrists, the camcorder my friends and I used to record dumb videos with one another. I keep photos of me from high school in my work bag, boys in tee-shirts under unbuttoned flannel, red eyes from the flash of disposable cameras. I keep the journal I wrote in at the boy's home after mom called the cops on me, had me arrested. I keep a note I wrote in it about when Mom dropped me off for the Scared Straight program at the county jail, laughed when I hesitated to get out of the car, told me I'd better not drop the soap. I keep things inside, too, but not because I want to. I keep the memory of her telling me she loves me but doesn't like me, the one of her sending me to school with SlimFasts until I lost weight, the one of her insisting I eat undercooked chicken she'd prepared, plated. I both remember it and relate to it whether I choose to or not, watch it back in my head day after day after day.

An hour or so into A Goofy Movie, Goofy and Max get out of the car and into an argument on the side of the road, but Goofy forgets to put on the parking brake, sending the car speeding down a mountain. The series of goofs ends with the two of them stranded atop their car, which floats along a gushing river, rock formations on either side. The gist of it is that they're stuck with one another without much of a way out, forcing them to reconcile. Their conversation climaxes when Max yells that he has his own life now, and Goofy, somber, replies, "I know that. I just wanted to be a part of it." It's the culmination of so much of what the film builds towards—Max's desire for independence, Goofy's worry that his son will become a delinquent, the pain of shifting family dynamics, and I think about how this would have hit if I'd watched it sooner. At 15, when I was arrested. At 22, when I moved away from my mom, started my own life, lost a hundred pounds and graduated college with a 4.0. At 26, 30, 31, when I came back, helped check my mom into rehab.

Two weeks after my daughter was born, I was holding her in the NICU when my dad called to let me know that my mom had died. I tightened my daughter's swaddle, tucked the feeding tubes and monitor cables beside her, and set her in her hospital-issued bassinet, signed myself out at the nursing station. I sanitized my hands, told the nurses I'd be back after a while, and they buzzed me out. My wife waited for me in the hallway. I stepped toward her then ran toward her, gripped her shirt in my fists, cried, told her what had happened. Told her that our daughter would never meet her nana, as my mom wanted to be called. We didn't know it at the time, but an autopsy later confirmed that she'd mixed some combination of alcohol and pills that her body couldn't handle. Or maybe we said we didn't know, but we did. It was always going to end in that sort of way, and I'm taken back to it when I see Goofy's defeat, the way his eyebrows lower, his shoulders slacken, his lip almost trembles. The desire to be a part of someone's life, to have fallen short.

A Goofy Movie ends with Goofy and Max returning home. Max has fulfilled his promise to Roxanne that he'd appear on TV at Powerline's concert in Los Angeles, but he admits to her that he'd lied, that he did what he said he would but that he never actually set out to do it at all, that he wanted to impress her. The moment's interrupted by Goofy himself, though, who due to a series of goofs, flies through the air and lands face first through the awning over Roxane's porch. Max introduces the two, introduces his dad, Goofy.

My wife and daughter come home two days after I watch A Goofy Movie. I give my daughter a bath that night, ask her about her weekend with my wife's parents. She tells me she missed me, and I tell her I missed her, too, that we'll read books together tonight, snuggle until she falls asleep. She asks me if I promise, and I tell her I do. I pull her out of the bath, set her on a towel, pull the hood over her head and tuck the sides around her. She's five now, but I picture her at two weeks when I wrap her like this. I pick her up to walk to her room but stop at a picture of my parents in the hall. They're young in it, maybe younger than I was when I met my wife. My mom is smiling, one hand on her hip, the other wrapped around my dad. Her teeth, her eyes, are white, bright, vibrant. Her hair, permed, blows across her face. They're standing on a gazebo on a beach in Florida not long after getting married. They're fulfilled, happy, alive.

"That's your Nana," I tell her. My daughter reaches out, runs a tiny finger across her face.

***

Adam Shaw's work has previously appeared in Pithead Chapel, Autofocus, HAD, and elsewhere. He lives with his wife and daughter in Louisville, Kentucky, and can be found online at theshawspot.com.

All I Want

Joe Bush

It's 5:13 PM on a Wednesday. I got off the bus at 3:17, was inside by 3:23, in my room by 3:24, had my Dreamcast on at 3:25, and, save for a bathroom break at 4:43, have been grinding runs in Crazy Taxi ever since 3:25 PM. This, if completed, will be my 19th full run today, my 25th total counting the six runs I aborted mid-session. Before B.D. Joe has begun to sit up from his pose lounging across the front seats, before the announcer has started the countdown, before the first jump cut of the pre-run cinematic, I've already tapped the A button and shifted my taxi into reverse.

I lift my controller to my chest and whip it down to my right thigh, tapping the B button during the swing and slamming the right trigger down on contact to time a perfect Crazy Boost. My taxi rockets off the sidewalk in time with the Offspring vocalist. *Yeah, yeah, yeah, yeah, yeah!* I speed past the first passengers. I skip orange and red emblems. Greens only. Yellows if desperate. I need the highest fares I can get. I slam hard on the left trigger to brake at the first cable car stop so I don't overshoot my first passenger or force her to jump out of the way and waste time running to get in. It's the pregnant woman in the green dress. She hops over my rear door into the back seat and tells me to take her to Popcorn Mania. I don't understand how a business that sells only popcorn can stay afloat. She must be having cravings. *Day after day, your whole life's a wreck / The powers that be just breathe down your neck.*

I slam down another Crazy Boost to launch off the flat and soar over the downward slope, hitting the ground with another to maintain speed. The whipping technique keeps my rhythm consistent: It goes lift, A-button, chest, B-button, thigh, right trigger, and it works every time. I barely fuck up Crazy Boosts anymore. I weave between drivers through the curve on the waterfront. My passenger stands up from the backseat and cheers. Cash register chimes pop from my TV speaker. I have the volume all the way up, but it's not loud enough to bother anybody if my door's shut. I kick up the ramp into the parking garage, slam down a

Crazy Boost as I drift, dodge a sedan backing out of its spot, and launch out over the Pizza Hut to the street below. I break my speed slamming my taxi's right side into a wall. There's probably a smoother way to do it but I've saved enough time that I can be rough. *You get no respect, you get no relief / You gotta stand up and yell out your piece.*

My best run today was the eleventh full run, thirteenth total, starting at 4:17 PM and finishing at 4:28 PM: nine passengers, $6,237.44 earned, 18th place, with a Class A license. My best ever finish was 12th, $7,057.04 earned, with a Class S License. It was 11:02pm on the Friday night of the third week of school, I wrote it down. I drift in front of the pink Popcorn Mania building and drop off my passenger. She high-fives B.D. Joe and runs off. 5 seconds are added to my timer. I try to reverse-Crazy Boost out but it doesn't work. My timing's not right on the reverse-Crazy Boosts yet. I speed past the priest under a yellow icon to the man in shorts and a ballcap under a green one. Take me to the baseball stadium, he says. *So back-off your rules and back off your jive / I'm sick of not living to stay alive.*

The front door whines open and slams shut downstairs. My bedroom walls shake. It's 5:17 PM. Mom's home a minute earlier than normal for a Wednesday. The red audio input plug-in swings from the impact, unused in my TV. It's technically supposed to be portable. My uncle gave it to me after the built-in antenna and battery door both broke when it fell off a table at a tailgate at a Twins game last fall. The tape deck sometimes ejects at random but it works enough for my purposes and no longer does for his. Mom would've never let me buy one with allowance money. She said having my own TV would just keep me cooped up in my room. I turn off-road at the curve to the church and boost uphill through the grass, launching up and over the helipad with another boost. My right index finger, both thumbs, and the fat of my right thigh all sting. The sun's going to break through my window and get in my eyes soon. I'll need to close my blinds once I finish this run. At this rate I'll get between two and three more runs in before dinner. I can hear mom and dad's voices downstairs. *How many tries is it gonna take / Til someone around you hears what you say?*

I drift around the hairpin in front of the train depot into the stadium parking lot. I avoid the impulse to jump off, which would land me in the middle of a row of parked buses and break my flow. I swerve through the cars in motion and cut through an aisle in the parking lot. The destination indicator flashes green in the distance. Their voices are getting louder. I pull up at the edge of the lot. My passenger high-fives B.D. Joe and jogs off to the ticket booth. I can't make out any words through the door but mom's voice is sharpening. Dad's isn't. 5 seconds are added to my timer. *I've said it before, I'll say it again / If you could just listen, then it might make sense.*

I pass a yellow and an orange icon to another green-icon passenger. I roll through the circle as I brake, he diverolls away from me and complains as he jogs up to my taxi. To the police station, he says. He's in a black tuxedo. I Crazy Boost off onto the freeway. These roads are narrow: two lanes of traffic, no sidewalks to cheat onto on the right side and one-way oncoming traffic on the left. I can only pass through small gaps in traffic or down the middle line if I need to risk it. I sneak between two vans on the middle line. I brake to avoid bumping a hatchback, but I just nick its left tail light. It spins out. My passenger shakes his fist at B.D. Joe and tells him to be more careful. *Leave me alone, not asking a lot, just don't wanna be controlled.*

I zip left around the hatchback and cut in front of an ambulance. Two semis stand ahead. If I boost at the perfect moment, I'll be able to split them. After that I'll be home free. *It's all I want.* I tap the stick left and position myself on the line. I lift back my controller, feel the memory card slot just tap my sternum as I tap the A-button, whip it forward, tap the B button on the swing, and slam down the right trigger as it punches into my thigh. My taxi speeds between the two trucks. *It's all I want.* Glass breaks downstairs. Mom's voice cuts through the walls carrying curse words and mine and dad's names. *It's all I want.* I clip the left semi. My taxi careens off to the left onto the opposite road. An ambulance t-bones my taxi. *It's all I want.* I tap the start button. The music stops. The house is silent.

I select "Retry." It's 5:19 PM on a Wednesday. If completed, this will be my 19th full run today.

***

Joe Bush teaches writing in Lawrence, Kansas. You can read his thoughts about soccer at www.scoresecondary.com and his thoughts on anything else at www.joebush.net.

Avoid the Noid

Jessica Gleason

A constant game of keep
away, he returns home, empty
apartment, grease-stained
cardboard boxes, strewn about,
crusts, maybe.

He peels off his signature
red suit, wrinkled from sweat,
smelling faintly of
mozzarella, and plops down,
parmesan bites in hand.

Turns the television
on, hoping to avoid advertisements,
having left work at work,
he's lonely. Binging
romantic comedies and
weeping a little each night.

Avoid, they said, and it
was catchy and it pays
the bills, but he'd trade
fast food infamy for real human
connection, any day.

***

Hawaiian-Italian author, Jessica Gleason, is a lover of horror and fantasy in their various shapes and forms and can usually be found penning gory tales deep into the night. She enjoys painting monsters with acrylics and singing a mean hair metal karaoke. Her daytime persona teaches college English and Communications in the American midwest. Her recent releases include ,The Dangerous Miss Ventriloquist,and “”The Fabulous Miss Fortune” (Evil Cookie Publishing, 2023) and “”Madison

Murphy, Wisconsin Weirdo"" (Champagne Books Group, 2023). For information on her projects, follow her on Instagram (@j.g.writes) where she hosts a monthly horror writer challenge, #WeWriteHorror. https://jgwrites.carrd.co

Hale-Bopp Bop

Edie Meade

Hale-Bopp Bop

[Capo on 2, A, G, Em, D, give'm hell Gunny]

disposable camera day, long tail
long-haul doppler fading away

me on drugs you on foot
meet me at the neon of the Pizza Hut

/

El Camino coming in hot, keep low
to the ground, coyote trot

me in front you in back
meet me at the dumpster of the Radio Shack

/

irrational exuberance, go on
twist your mood ring give it a chance

me on mix tape you in memory
meet me at the end of the century

/

[Chorus]
send an Astronomical Telegram
check on Frank Black, tell a friend

we found Heaven's Gate closing in
the San Diego sky

***

Edie Meade is a writer and one-half of songwriting duo The Oxbow Estate in Petersburg, Virginia.

Gravitational Kinks

Katie Beswick

No binary between death & life;
no certain end. A continuum.

A tile buckles
loosening space time;

you can pull it back
feeling its cool against your palm.

Time flops out from the cavity,
like a paper map laid flat;

paths marked in coded colours.
Countries as years; cities are hours.

In the foreign present,
new world spices burn my tongue.

Weird music spills from sleek cars in thumps.
I lean into that map, set myself

on the yellow path back to 2001:
home country. Its scent of weed

smoke hot in Gib's red Fiesta.
We were all alive then,

nodding at garage lyrics
played over pirate radio.

Streets unrazed; familiar.
The air spoke our own language.

***

Katie Beswick is a writer from south east London. Recent poetry has appeared in Rattle, The Waxed Lemon, English: Journal of the English Association, Ink Sweat & Tears. Her debut chapbook is Plumstead Pram Pushers (Red Ogre 2024). Her forthcoming hybrid book of memior, poetry and art criticism is Slags on Stage (Routledge 2025).

I want to go home.

Sarah R. New

I want to go home.

Except, when I say I want to go home, what I mean is that I yearn for those long summer days where the sky was always clear, and the sun shone down. You'd have a Mr Whippy in hand, the ones with the flake and the raspberry sauce. The Olympics was on, and we spent hours watching gymnastics and diving while making an ill-fated scarecrow. Gordon Brown was the Prime Minister and you didn't know anything about him, only that he had incredible eyebrows and that he seemed a bit boring but that you were sure he was probably quite nice? There's a recession but you don't even know what that is, and even if you did, you still probably wouldn't understand it. Your afternoons are filled with sneaky sessions of Neopets on the family computer, and fighting with your sister, and learning to bake with your mum.

It is 2008 and no one is sick yet, and no one has died yet, and you don't know the horrors this world can bring. The disability that lurks in your body has not yet taken hold, and you are still able to run, jump, leap, without the threat of a dislocation. You are young and naïve on the cusp of teenagehood, and you still believe that the world is good, and you are safe. You are safe here. You are safe in your body. You are loved.

I want to go home.

***

Sarah R. New (she/her) has recently been published in journals including the Hoogly Review, Wishbone Words, Gastropoda, and in Broken Olive Branches, a Palestinian charity anthology. Her Gothic horror novella, Amissis Liberis, was published by Alien Buddha Press in May 2024. Her travel memoir, The Great European Escape is available for free from https://sarahrnew.wordpress.com/.

Instructions for Avoiding INS, 1997

Arvin Ramgoolam

Make a decision and make it fast. Stay or run. Local cops stop you, you stay, talk, hope they've got some piece of humanity in them, rattling around like the perfect glass ball in a can of spray paint.

Pray, pray, pray your immigrant ass is a bigger headache than they are willing to deal with. If it's INS—youfuckingrun.

If you're going to run, know your exits. Plan your route. The adrenaline is going
to kick, so you'll have that to work with.

Boss is tired of Americans. Calling in late, calling in sick. You do neither and do it for less money. Cash.

1) Make sure one person knows your status so if you get caught they can call your family, get a lawyer, and tell your scuzzy roommate he's not getting that roll of bills you normally hand over a few days before rent is due, because you're good like that.

They call it, Immigration and Naturalization Service, like they're going to help you out. But you've heard about Krome Detention Center on the edge of the rotting Everglades. Alligators have the decency to stalk you because it's in their nature, hiding in plain sight, their unkind eyes, like marbles, above the water as they slowly approach, giving you time to see them.

2) When you run, you've got to have a spot that would make it hard to find you. Low profile, no profile.

Boss hires you because he's cheap. Trusts you because he knows you're scared of law enforcement. Laughs when he pays you your measly weekly, and can't say shit because you're the one who'll be in trouble if someone finds out.

3) Speak—good—english. Pronounce everything exactly. Yes, not

yea. Pardon me, not 'scuse me. You realize this in high school during a Business Leaders of America meeting, before you start looking for your social security number. Language is your first line of defense. The speed you can run is your last.

4) Stay clean. No drugs. Drink only to fit in.

Laugh like you have nothing to fear, the way you've heard Americans laugh when you've ordered a cheap beer and let it sit on the bar after three sips. Laugh like it was a joke when you got into a bunch of Ivy League schools and then were told you couldn't go because you didn't have papers. Be afraid of everything, including the hospital. You're not worried about a bill. You're afraid they'll see that passport ID and call your ass in.

5) Fear is your friend.

Lay low until you can move on. Move out. Have a plan, motherfucker. No planes. Look for that next job. Become a hunter of human sympathy. Play the Green Card Lottery every three months. You have no luck, but they don't know that.

If you can outrun them, you'll have another day out of the detention center and away from the deportation judge. You can't go back to the country you came from because you don't know how to make money there. Your good American English scrubbed too much of your homeland out of your mouth and you'll be a man without a country when you can't even sound like you belong there.

You thought Clinton would be a cool president. Your parents tell you, Bush is better for us, but you don't understand what they're trying to say and won't for years. When Clinton declares war on your immigrant ass, you'll start to think they were right. You don't think it now, but you are brave.

You look at the door all the time, ready to bolt out the back. You see black shirts, white men, dark glasses, you pause. Police? INS? A fraternity? You play that game everyday. You don't know how long it will last. Roll the dice on the Immigrant Diversity Program.

Boss is all Rush Limbaugh, this guy on the radio that really speaks to him, and says things he's been told not to say. Revels in hearing about how hard it is for immigrants the way children realize ants have no defense against their dirty sneakers. He connects nothing to you. The good English and subservience make it easy for him to forget.
When it's INS, and you're young, you've got to have a plan, no family to look out for, you run.

6) Stay away from women if you're a man, stay away from men if you're a woman.

If you're gay, keep that secret as tight as your status because they're keeping a secret too, and that—my friend—is too many secrets for one home to hold.

7) If you find love; the kind of love that won't report you when they get jealous, the kind of love that doesn't repel when you tell them why you pay for everything in cash, the kind of love that offers to marry you and help you get your papers even if they fall out of love with you, the kind of love you kiss in front of the justice of the peace as you hold your precious passport and anxiously wait for someone to say you can't do this, or love that holds you at night and makes you feel like you belong somewhere, then hold on to that because you won't have much to hold on to.

Until the day you are told you don't have a social security number, a green card, a chance, you never know yourself as anything but American. Learn all the history including the dirty parts. More history than your own home country.

8) Learn to quote all three Star Wars movies and this will help more than you know.

Say the Pledge of Allegiance everyday in school like you meant it, and finally cry when you say it at your citizenship ceremony in 30 years. Follow these instructions and you'll make it. Where? You don't know, but you sure as hell won't be in Krome Detention Center.

***

Arvin Ramgoolam is the co-owner of Townie Books in Crested Butte, Colorado. His words can be found in The Normal School, the Jellyfish Review, AAWW, and ANMLY.

T9 Dating

Elisabeth Rourke

The world was divided: Those who had smartphones and those who did not. Ashley was one of the few millennials unwilling to be swayed, because the item in her purse she couldn't possibly live without was a spiral-bound day planner, not a skinny, black rectangle.

Perhaps online dating was more socially accepted in fancy places like Manhattan, but in the Midwestern suburbs, there was a stigma—a hushed, judgment-filled buzz that had many who'd entered these websites lying through their teeth (*We met in line at Starbucks, the aisles of Borders, "Daiquiri Night" at T.G.I. Fridays*).

Growing up watching *Sex and the City*, Ashley (a total Carrie) thought she wanted something casual. Maybe a fling. A free meal at the very least. The breakup of her seven-year relationship with her high school "sweetheart" was fresh, and at the time, she had considered herself only mildly damaged. But as she watched Seven-Year load his crap onto a moving dolly from the bonfire-like pile she'd gathered at the center of her apartment—a tube television the size of a small human, an overly masculine entertainment console, and plastic grocery bags filled with Xbox games, a bong, two paintball magazines, and a past-due Netflix DVD of *Dude, Where's My Car?*—she was struck by a renewed sense of confidence when it came to setting up an online dating profile.

How bad could it be?

But in a world where the Apple 3GS was all the rage, among other trends that she'd assumed would certainly pass— *#emojis, #gifs, #selfies* — it became increasingly apparent that Ashley, who thought she knew what she wanted, didn't know what she wanted at all.

Day one of Ashley's dating inbox held three solid potentials and one, six-foot-four Italian man (PastaBravo12) whose muscular thigh was the size of her torso—Ashley, measuring at five-foot-two, deemed the physics of this match to be unsuitable (painful, even), and as much as she enjoyed eating pasta, she declined Pasta Bravo's romantic advance by not returning his wink.

Potential #1:

Potential #1 messaged Ashley sweet things. No creepy vibes. Steady job. Good-looking. Asked get-to-know-ya questions and liked to text things like, *"We should totally get coffee sometime."* And each time that kind of text came through, Ashley would pull out her spiral-bound day planner and flip to the week.

4-4-4, 6, 0, 3-3-3, 5-5-5, 3-3, 9-9, 4-4-4, 2-2, 5-5, 3-3, 0, 9, 4-4, 2, 8, 0, 9, 6-6-6, 7-7-7, 5-5, 7-7-7-7, 0, 3-3-3, 6-6-6, 9-9-9? *(I'm flexible, what works for you?)*

…

…

Two days later: "Hey hun. Been thinking about you. We should go out for drinks soon."

4-4-4, 6, 0, 3-3-3, 7-7-7, 3-3-, 0, 8, 6-6-6, 6, 6-6-6, 7-7-7, 7-7-7, 6-6-6, 9. *(I'm free tomorrow.)*

…

…

…

Three nights later: "Hey beautiful."

Ashley started to make excuses for Potential #1; he seemed polite and was steadily employed (or so his profile had claimed). *One more chance?* She stared at #1's text message *"Hey beautiful."*

Ashley snapped her flip phone closed; she chose not to reply. She ignored a second text as well and when she didn't, #1 called her a bitch and said he was deleting her number.

Potential #2:

Funny. Really funny. Maybe he wasn't that funny. Maybe he just quoted *Anchorman* a lot. #2 lived at home still—not that there was anything wrong with that; they were in their early twenties—but Ashley didn't live at home—she had a budget, lived in an apartment without roommates, had a five-year plan, a day planner—and the idea of having sex with someone, like Seven-year, who still had their mother doing laundry for them was a total turnoff.

Potential #3:

Very hot. Abercrombie hot. Chiseled abs, tan skin. *"They have sexy drinks for sexy ladies*" was his line when Ashley had inquired about the local bar #3 suggested they go to. Ashley was new to dating, yes, but "*sexy drinks for sexy ladies*" gave off the impression that perhaps the chiseled abs of #3's photo was false advertising.

Ashley's gut told her to distance herself from this conversation, but ever-persistent #3 texted and texted and texted. "Hey, yo—U up? Can't wait to buy that sexy ass a sexy drink."

Ashley was, indeed, up—but to quote Randy Jackson, "*That's gonna be a no for me, dawg.*" She flipped open her phone and started to type: 7-7-7-7, 6-6-6, 7-7-7, 7-7-7, 9-9-9, 0, 8, 4-4-, 4-4-4, 7-7-7-7, 0, 3, 6-6-6, 3-3, 7-7-7-7, 6-6, 8, 0, 9, 6-6-6, 7-7-7, 5-5, 0, 3-3-3, 6-6-6, 7-7-7, 0, 6, 3-3. *(Sorry, this doesn't work for me.)*

Having learned her lesson from Potential #1, Ashley blocked #3's phone number and dating profile before he could respond.

Alone in her apartment on a Saturday night, wearing sweatpants and eating a cold slice of deep-dish pizza, Ashley began questioning the validity of this type of service. Would it be easier to meet someone at a bar? What type of man would she find there? Online dating took the guesswork out of the many questions she had—*Was he employed? Did he have goals? Did his picture look like he might smell like patchouli IRL?*

In hindsight, Ashley may have over-filtered her options considering her claim of only wanting a free meal, maybe a fling, if she were lucky. Was she being too picky? Or did she no longer feel like settling? That perhaps this seven-year relationship she'd recently removed herself from was lesson enough to learn that she'd deserved more than a one-nighter. Deserved more than what these boys without day planners could offer.

Perhaps an older man was what Ashley needed. Someone more established, someone with a 401k, someone who didn't drive a beater that smelled like day-old McDonald's.

Ashley searched. She clicked through photos. Scanned the profiles—Legally separated. *Has children. Looked too much like Wall Street.*

Only two days remained until Ashley's credit card would be charged for another month of online dating, and she missed basic cable more than she wanted a free meal.

But on the last day, and amid messages that began with *Hey baby, You're hot*, and *Great tits*, a new kind of subject line hit Ashley's dating inbox.

Potential #4:

"I hope this doesn't come off as weird, but I think you're the female version of myself."

The four short paragraphs that followed were well-worded. No grammar or spelling errors. And considering the garbage littering her inbox—pictures of naked torsos hinting towards a trail of pubic hair—this articulate email was practically Shakespeare. *"I wasn't matched with you,"* #4 had written. *"Not really, at least."*

He went on to explain that Ashley was but a tiny thumbnail at the bottom of an email claiming he had run out of matches— He, too, had over-filtered his settings. *"You were right there, at the bottom, next to a girl from Tallahassee. You were the only person from Illinois, so I clicked on you and read your profile. I'd like to get to know you more."*

They began chatting daily on Skype; their Yahoo emails to one another were hidden beneath spreadsheets on their work computers.

#4 was gainfully employed, completing an engineering degree, and just like Ashley, lived on his own without roommates.

#4 was funny but not crass, had tasteful tattoos, played the guitar, came from a good family, and preferred dogs over cats.

#4 had two older sisters—just like Ashley—claimed to know how to sew a button, listed all the places he'd like to travel to someday, valued work ethic over house parties.

They talked about their past relationships. They traded music and liked the same movies. She laughed at his jokes, and he laughed at hers. But as much as Ashley wanted a date—a real date—she kept her spiral-bound day planner closed on her desk.

Until… Ashley's flip phone buzzed from her pocket—a text from #4: "Enough chatting. Can I take you out to dinner?"

Ashley screamed and danced around her apartment. She waited six minutes to respond. She played it cool: 9-9-9, 3-3, 2, 4-4, 0, 7-7-7-7, 8-8, 7-7-7, 3-3. *(Sure.)*

Within the same minute, #4 texted back. "Mind if I call you? I really hate texting."

Ashely high-fived herself. She danced around her apartment some more. She waited two minutes to respond. She played it cool: 9-9-9, 3-3, 2, 4-4, 0, 7-7-7-7, 8-8, 7-7-7, 3-3. *(Sure.)*

On their Razr flip phones, they discussed restaurant options. #4 lived nearly an hour away with traffic, but insisted he pick Ashley up at her front door—maybe with flowers, he hinted.

Ashley's fingertips slowly skimmed the pages of her spiral-bound day planner, flipping it open to the current week. This felt solid. This felt good. If only she could be sure. "I'm free Tuesday," she said.

There was a pause.

#4 was thinking.

"Let me double-check my planner," he said, "But I think it's a date.

***

Elisabeth Rourke is a freelance content writer and editor and also works as a professional editorial assistant. Her work has been accepted into StoryStudio Chicago, where she is actively working on her second novel. She lives in the Chicagoland suburbs with her husband and Wheaten terrier, Rigby.

Youth!

Romy Rhoads Ewing

Red bulls with sickly thick sugary-sweet
Syrup at the all-ages show, you and me armed with
Plastic film canisters filled with cheap vodka from
Cheap plastic bottles, an emblem of St. Basil's
Cathedral wears as we stray from it, burn the
Proof, our letters and our fingertips, sprouting wings and
Baptized in sludge, stuck together eternally.

A collage of
What my parents find
Cleaning out my childhood
Closet–I beg you
To alchemize me
Into something less simple.

***

Romy Rhoads Ewing (she/they) is a writer and photographer from Sacramento, California. Her work has appeared or is forthcoming in Bullshit Lit, fifth wheel press, BRAWL, HAD, Querencia Press, No-where Girl Collective, Anti-Heroin Chic, Major 7th Magazine, ME-MEZINE, persephone's fruit, UC Davis's Open Ceilings Magazine, and Genrepunk Magazine. Her debut chapbook, please stay, was published by Bottlecap Press in 2024. Romy, their work, and further information can be found online at www.romyrhoadsewing.xyz.

The Geometry of Darkness

Spencer Nitkey

The Geometry of Darkness: An Ode to the Gamecube Introduction Screen

The sun's great waves ebb and leave darkness. Promise whispers from the star-dappled cloth of night. On the carpet, a light body, half-boyed half-manned, all roil and fear finds respite. Escape.
The mediated evening crawls on cathode-ray legs, pre-fluorescence, across the floor. Watch. The screen shadows the high pile rug. What makes the world disappear?
A new light bursts, bright and eager. Have you smelled the meat of a kill crisped on hot stone? Have you felt the carry of an undertow and let it take you? Have the highways blurred into movie theater screens, your eyes both projector and receiver of the projection? Yes. Remember, the green and yellow blur of cornfields and your dreaming. Of her? Of him? Of both?
This too is erased as the light converts, like the sun before it, to an insistent darkness. A black screen is not true darkness. It is something else. Sleep is not death, though it approximates it. Sleep is not death because you wake up. The black screen is not darkness because it insists you see it. Nothing, you learned recently in a large book from your cousin, not even light, its particles and waves, can escape from a blackhole.
You do not notice your doing it, but you hold your breath. The black screen is a promise. A promise of oblivion, of a lack of body, of a lack of mind. It is not darkness, it is everything, so much you can't possibly imagine ever making sense of it.
Sense is made, though not by you.
A cube in the dark, an atom in the void, a thought in the back of your mind that comes from somewhere else to put a hole in the wall or scream into a pillow, a cube in the dark. Curved and purple, its edges enhance its geometric perfection. It falls from the sky, which is the top of the TV, which is the cornfield, which is your own wants reflected back at you.

It falls and you remember that voids can be filled. But with what? It lands and signals a reminder. Within the dark promise it flashes a large cube. Opaque walls and blacklines for edges flash, you almost miss it, but you never do. Within the crowded black, the evening's potential, the ghost of an image, phantasms into view then vanishes. Rapture. The cube walks over itself in straight lines. It leaves square footprints, separated by thin lines, in the dark as if in snow. Where it fell stays blank, but its first step, its first turn to the upper left insists. You can, it whispers, make marks upon the darkness. This is a promise though it seems a threat.

Each step sends a single, sonorous note. Two steps, two cubes, then a rotation, as it continues its walk. It is tracing the outline of the larger image, the ghost. Three steps then another rotation, this time a dripping downward. Three more across the center of the screen to the right, then another rotation, a mirror of its previous steps, then up by three until—

You expect a gentle turn, for the cube's path to end where it began, to close the loop, to make a larger cube. It does not notice your wanting, nor care. It twists sharply, at the first right angle the cube has taken. You smirk because it has made the letter G.

The wandering cube that has torn open the darkness jumps into the air, toward you, growing large and feral. Teeth in the darkness. If it keeps going it will fill the screen, fall out of the screen. You can see its shining purple mass expanding into your world until it swallows you, and your mother, and the neighbors barking husky, and your school, and the pharmacy you steal headphones from, everything in the whole world. You wouldn't mind, you think.

But it stops. Freezes in the air. Pauses for a glitched moment of non-motion. Hitched like the breath you realize now you've been holding. Taut and ringing. Tension is where the music lies.

Then the descent, a straight line down, falling into the center of the outlined cube. It falls and you exhale with it. It lands and chimes.

A word appears below "Gamecube." Had you forgotten, in this warm void, words and letters. Maybe.

Then, the final transformation. The many steps cohere. The lines between them vanish, smooth into one another. The outline sheens and shimmers. The first metallic hint.

It begins. From here you are taken to another world. The promise of that black is fulfilled, but that is incidental. You remember this, the darkness, the geometry of darkness, the spreading cornfields, the back of your eyelids as you fall asleep more than any game you play. You can carve a path through it. You can leave footprints in the dark snow. You can burst to life through darkness and shine. You can. You wonder, as the screen fades and you are taken from this liminal place, whether or not you will. But you can.
END

***

Spencer Nitkey is a writer living in Philadelphia. His writing has appeared, or is forthcoming, in Apex Magazine, Diabolical Plots, trampset, Lightspeed Magazine, Flash Fiction Online, The Dissappointed Housewife, and others. He was a finalist for the 2023 Eugie Foster Memorial Award in Short Fiction and has been nominated for the Pushcart Prize, Best Small Fictions, and the Rhysling Award.

Author Index

Issue 1

Issue 2

Issue 3

Issue 4

www.ingramcontent.com/pod-product-compliance
Lightning Source LLC
Chambersburg PA
CBHW070405200726
48294CB00003B/1103

* 9 7 8 1 7 3 3 5 7 0 7 2 5 *